JavaScript Projects for Kids

Gear up for a roller-coaster ride into the world of
JavaScript and programming with this easy-to-follow,
fun, and entertaining project-based guide

Syed Omar Faruk Towaha

[PACKT] open source*
PUBLISHING   community experience distilled

BIRMINGHAM - MUMBAI

JavaScript Projects for Kids

First published: January 2016

Production reference: 1220116

Published by Packt Publishing Ltd.
Livery Place
35 Livery Street
Birmingham B3 2PB, UK.

ISBN 978-1-78528-717-6

www.packtpub.com

Credits

Author
Syed Omar Faruk Towaha

Reviewer
Johnathan Iannotti

Commissioning Editor
Veena Pagare

Acquisition Editor
Aaron Lazar

Content Development Editor
Sachin Karnani

Technical Editor
Manthan Raja

Copy Editor
Vibha Shukla

Project Coordinator
Nikhil Nair

Proofreader
Safis Editing

Indexer
Mariammal Chettiyar

Graphics
Disha Haria

Jason Monteiro

Production Coordinator
Arvindkumar Gupta

Cover Work
Arvindkumar Gupta

About the Author

Syed Omar Faruk Towaha has degrees in physics and computer engineering. He is a technologist, tech speaker, and physics lover from Shahjalal University of Science and Technology (SUST), Sylhet. He has a passion for programming, tech writing, and physics experiments.

His recent books include *Easy Circuits for Kids*, *Fundamentals of Ruby*, and *How You Should Design Algorithms*. He is an Oracle-certified professional developer currently involved with a number of projects that serve both physics and computer architecture.

He is the president of one of the largest astronomical organizations (Copernicus Astronomical Memorial of SUST (CAM-SUST)) in Bangladesh. He also volunteers for Mozilla as a representative.

I wish to take the opportunity to thank the staff at Packt Publishing for their commitment and hard work, especially Sachin Karnani (Content Development Editor), Aaron Lazar (Acquisition Editor), and Nikhil Nair (Project Coordinator). They got numerous reviews, kept the book on track, and helped me in many ways. I really appreciate their input. I also wish to thank Johnathan Iannotti (Reviewer) for his constructive criticism and helpful comments.

Table of Contents

www.PacktPub.com

Support files, eBooks, discount offers, and more

For support files and downloads related to your book, please visit www.PacktPub.com.

Did you know that Packt offers eBook versions of every book published, with PDF and ePub files available? You can upgrade to the eBook version at www.PacktPub.com and as a print book customer, you are entitled to a discount on the eBook copy. Get in touch with us at service@packtpub.com for more details.

At www.PacktPub.com, you can also read a collection of free technical articles, sign up for a range of free newsletters and receive exclusive discounts and offers on Packt books and eBooks.

https://www2.packtpub.com/books/subscription/packtlib

Do you need instant solutions to your IT questions? PacktLib is Packt's online digital book library. Here, you can search, access, and read Packt's entire library of books.

Why subscribe?
- Fully searchable across every book published by Packt
- Copy and paste, print, and bookmark content
- On demand and accessible via a web browser

Free access for Packt account holders

If you have an account with Packt at www.PacktPub.com, you can use this to access PacktLib today and view 9 entirely free books. Simply use your login credentials for immediate access.

About the Reviewer

Johnathan Iannotti is a software engineer and geek on an epic journey of life. His experience spans 15 years of technology solutions for start-ups, financial companies, healthcare, and military. He is passionate about web technology and has been creating hybrid apps since their inception. A full-stack developer by trade, he loves UX/UI, frontend development, and mobile.

He works for USAA, creating mobile applications for over 27,000 employees that serve their military membership. He is also a combat veteran having served almost a decade in the United States Army.

Johnathan spends his time innovating, coding, and making the best of it all. When he's not plugged in, he spends as much time as he can with his beautiful wife and two children who make it all possible. <3

Follow Johnathan on Twitter at @notticode or visit his website at http://johnforhire.com/.

Preface

As you can guess from the title of the book, this book is designed and set up for kids so that they can teach themselves JavaScript and create some projects using JavaScript.

By abstracting the core web programming in an unparalleled way, JavaScript changed websites and web apps forever. Boring static websites and non-interactive websites have now become quite awesome with the touch of JavaScript. Using JavaScript, you can develop web applications, even smartphone applications too, quickly without compromising quality. You can be very productive and deal with almost no configuration on your hardware and software if you start playing with JavaScript. Please remember that this is not a reference book, but you can learn every basic concepts of JavaScript from it. So, for the kids aged 10 and above, this will be a perfect book to discover the world of JavaScript.

What this book covers

Chapter 1, *Exploring JavaScript in the Console*, discusses JavaScript and the JavaScript Development Environment, including Google Developer Tools. We will install the necessary software and print a few simple lines of code in this chapter.

Chapter 2, *Solving Problems Using JavaScript*, covers JavaScript fundamentals from the main syntax to some easy commands in the console. We will learn how variables work and what can be achieved with arithmetic operators. We will also run some simple commands to solve problems inside the console.

Chapter 3, *Introducing HTML and CSS*, will make real use of JavaScript and will cover HTML, which empowers the readers to make use of JavaScript not only in the console but also in the browser's view. We will also explain the basics of CSS, such as CSS selectors, and CSS layouts.

Chapter 4, *Diving a Bit Deeper*, covers some of the more advanced features that JavaScript offers. We discuss for and while loops, if statements, and switches-case.

Chapter 5, Ahoy! Sailing into Battle, teaches us how to develop the famous game, Battleship. Building upon what we've learned in the previous chapters, the tiny tots will learn to put this information into use.

Chapter 6, Exploring the Benefits of jQuery, is all about jQuery, a famous JavaScript library, and the advantages of using it.

Chapter 7, Introducing the Canvas, discusses HTML canvas, and we will learn how we can use it on our projects.

Chapter 8, Building Rat-man!, teaches us to develop a famous game, Pac-Man, except there is a rat, some cats, and lots and lots of cheese balls to eat! ;)

Chapter 9, Tidying up Your Code Using OOP, teaches object-oriented programming (OOP) and discusses how JavaScript is an OOP language.

Chapter 10, Possibilities, shows the reader what is possible using the skills they have developed reading this book.

What you need for this book

Throughout this book, we have used Google Chrome as our browser to run our JavaScript code on the console. We wrote our code using Atom, a famous text editor. You can use any modern web browser and text editor, but I highly recommend that you to use these open source software to make any of the projects discussed in this book.

Who this book is for

If you've never written code before, or you are completely new to the world of web programming, then this book is the right choice for you. This book is for kids of age 10 years and above and adults who are completely new to the world of programming and want to get introduced to programming.

Conventions

In this book, you will find a number of text styles that distinguish between different kinds of information. Here are some examples of these styles and an explanation of their meaning.

Code words in text, database table names, folder names, filenames, file extensions, pathnames, dummy URLs, user input, and Twitter handles are shown as follows: "Click the `AtomSetup.exe` file to get started with installing Atom."

A block of code is set as follows:

```
document.write("Hello");
document.write("World");
document.write("!");
```

New terms and **important words** are shown in bold. Words that you see on the screen, for example, in menus or dialog boxes, appear in the text like this: "Clicking the **Next** button moves you to the next screen."

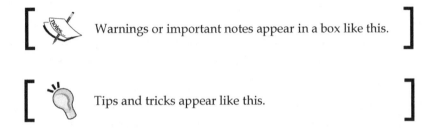

> Warnings or important notes appear in a box like this.

> Tips and tricks appear like this.

Reader feedback

Feedback from our readers is always welcome. Let us know what you think about this book—what you liked or disliked. Reader feedback is important for us as it helps us develop titles that you will really get the most out of.

To send us general feedback, simply e-mail feedback@packtpub.com, and mention the book's title in the subject of your message.

If there is a topic that you have expertise in and you are interested in either writing or contributing to a book, see our author guide at www.packtpub.com/authors.

Customer support

Now that you are the proud owner of a Packt book, we have a number of things to help you to get the most from your purchase.

Downloading the example code

You can download the example code files from your account at http://www.packtpub.com for all the Packt Publishing books you have purchased. If you purchased this book elsewhere, you can visit http://www.packtpub.com/support and register to have the files e-mailed directly to you.

Downloading the color images of this book

We also provide you with a PDF file that has color images of the screenshots/diagrams used in this book. The color images will help you better understand the changes in the output. You can download this file from `https://www.packtpub.com/sites/default/files/downloads/JavaScript_Projects_for_Kids_ColorImages.pdf`.

Errata

Although we have taken every care to ensure the accuracy of our content, mistakes do happen. If you find a mistake in one of our books—maybe a mistake in the text or the code—we would be grateful if you could report this to us. By doing so, you can save other readers from frustration and help us improve subsequent versions of this book. If you find any errata, please report them by visiting `http://www.packtpub.com/submit-errata`, selecting your book, clicking on the **Errata Submission Form** link, and entering the details of your errata. Once your errata are verified, your submission will be accepted and the errata will be uploaded to our website or added to any list of existing errata under the Errata section of that title.

To view the previously submitted errata, go to `https://www.packtpub.com/books/content/support` and enter the name of the book in the search field. The required information will appear under the **Errata** section.

Piracy

Piracy of copyrighted material on the Internet is an ongoing problem across all media. At Packt, we take the protection of our copyright and licenses very seriously. If you come across any illegal copies of our works in any form on the Internet, please provide us with the location address or website name immediately so that we can pursue a remedy.

Please contact us at `copyright@packtpub.com` with a link to the suspected pirated material.

We appreciate your help in protecting our authors and our ability to bring you valuable content.

Questions

If you have a problem with any aspect of this book, you can contact us at `questions@packtpub.com`, and we will do our best to address the problem.

1
Exploring JavaScript in the Console

Before we start talking about lines of codes, objects, variables, and so on, we need to know what JavaScript is. JavaScript is a programming language that is used to add interactivities to the web pages and build web applications. Static websites are not very popular these days, therefore, we use JavaScript to make our websites interactive.

Some people also call it a scripting language as it is an easy language and does not require compilers like other languages. JavaScript was not designed as a general purpose programming language, it was designed to manipulate web pages. You can write a desktop application using JavaScript. JavaScript can also access your machine's hardware. You can try making a desktop application with a **software development kit (SDK)** such as PhoneGap for mobile or the Microsoft app SDK for desktop. The JavaScript codes are interpreted on web pages and then run by a browser. Any modern Internet browser, for example Firefox, Safari, Google Chrome, UC Browser, Opera, and so on, supports JavaScript.

A *compiler* is a computer program that processes codes and turns them to machine language. Making a website *interactive* means adding features that are controlled by the users to the website. For example, online registration forms, online calculator, and so on. The *Static* website has fixed objects and contents and it displays the same information to all the visitors.

Basically, JavaScript is included on an HTML page or written on a separate file that has a .js extension. If you know nothing about HTML, don't worry as you will learn about it in *Chapter 3, Introducing HTML and CSS*. So, where can you use JavaScript?

The answer is simple, you can do the following:

- You can create an active user interface.
- You can control web browsers.
- You can validate user inputs (if they are typed wrong).
- You can create custom web pages that can pop up on the browser, holding information or images.
- You can create dynamic pages without **Common Gateway Interface** (**CGI**). CGI is used by the web servers to process a browser's information.

 The thing that you should remember is JavaScript is not Java, the programming language developed by Sun Microsystem.

Throughout this book, we will use **Google Chrome** as the default browser and **Atom** as the text editor.

If you do not have these two software already installed on your computer, it is necessary to download and install them.

We will use the Atom text editor as it is a cross-platform editor, has a built-in package manager, does smart autocompletion, and has a lot of other advantages.

Installing Google Chrome

To install Google Chrome go to `http://www.google.com/chrome` and click **Download now**, as shown in the following screenshot:

Then press the **Accept and Install** button, as shown in the following screenshot:

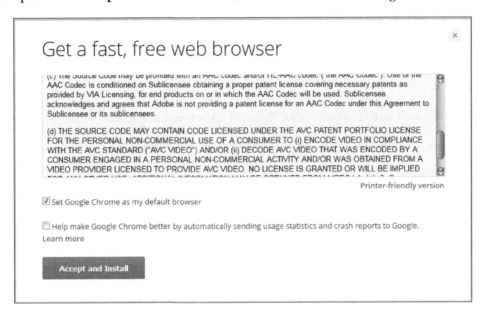

The installation will be completed depending on your network speed and machine's hardware configurations.

 Uncheck **Set Google Chrome as my default browser** if you don't want to use Google Chrome as your default browser.

Installing Atom

To install the Atom text editor, follow the https://atom.io/ link and press **Download Windows Installer**, as shown in the following screenshot:

A file called `AtomSetup.exe` will start downloading.

Click on the `AtomSetup.exe` file to get started with installing Atom.

[🔍 Make sure that you give the administrative rights while installing it for better performance.]

Atom will launch automatically after the installation is completed.

If you are on another platform, use the **Other platforms** link:

- If you are a Mac user, go to the `https://github.com/atom/atom/releases/latest` link and download the `atom-X.X.X-full.nupkg` file, where `X.X.X` is the version number of Atom. Install it by double-clicking on the file.

- If you are an Ubuntu user, you can follow the `https://github.com/atom/atom/releases/latest` link and download the `atom-amd64.deb` file. After downloading it, launch your **Terminal** in the same folder, where you placed the file after downloading it. Then, write the following code:

  ```
  sudo dpkg --install atom-amd64.deb
  ```

  You may need the administrative password to install it. After the installation is complete, you can run Atom from the Terminal by typing `Atom` and pressing *Enter*.

Chrome Developer Tools

Let's take a look at the **Chrome Developer Tools** that are used for JavaScript, specially the *console*. Since Google Chrome is downloaded and installed on your machine, open the Google Chrome browser, go to the menu (on the right-hand top corner), hover on **More tools** and select **Developer tools**, as shown in the following screenshot:

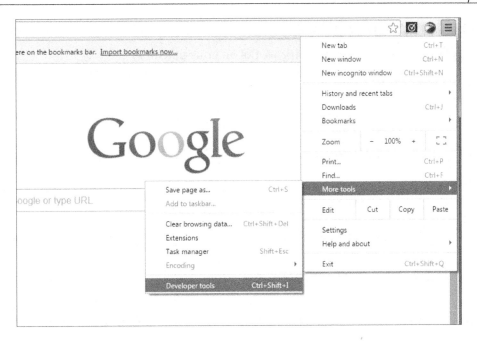

You will see the following tools:

- **Elements**
- **Network**
- **Sources**
- **Timeline**
- **Profiles**
- **Resources**
- **Audits**
- **Console**

Our first program

Now, let's check whether JavaScript works on your machine.

From the tools, select **Console**. If you cannot find **Console**, click on the **>>** symbol, as follows:

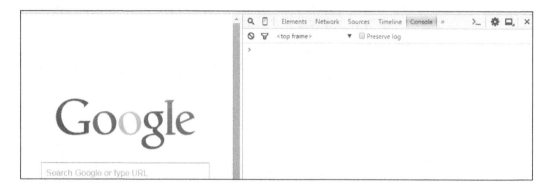

Once your console is open, type the following code and hit *Enter* on your keyboard:

```
document.write("Hello World");
```

If you can see the output on the left-hand side panel as shown in the following, then you have successfully configured JavaScript on your browser:

The output that you will see is as follows:

Hello World

Congratulations!

If you cannot see the text, check your code or install Google Chrome with administrative rights.

You can also click on the gear button of your console. Check whether **Disable JavaScript** is unchecked:

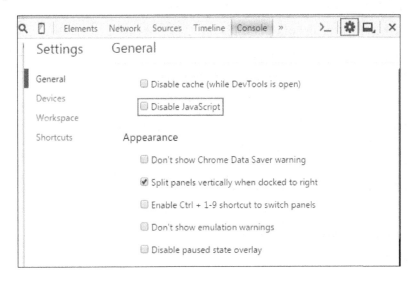

You can also debug your JavaScript codes using this tool.

If you type anything wrong; consider that you forgot the inverted commas of the `Hello World` string, you will get the following errors:

```
> document.write(Hello World)
⊗ ▼Uncaught SyntaxError: missing ) after argument list                      VM1681:2
      at Object.InjectedScript._evaluateOn (<anonymous>:904:140)
      at Object.InjectedScript._evaluateAndWrap (<anonymous>:837:34)
      at Object.InjectedScript.evaluate (<anonymous>:693:21)
   InjectedScript._evaluateOn          @ VM1539:904
   InjectedScript._evaluateAndWrap @ VM1539:837
   InjectedScript.evaluate             @ VM1539:693
```

To speed up writing your codes, you may learn some keyboard shortcuts for both console and Atom text editor.

Here are few keyboard shortcuts for console:

- *Ctrl + L*: Clear console
- *Tab*: Autocomplete common prefix
- Right arrow: Accept suggestion

- *Ctrl + U*: Clear console prompt
- *Up/Down*: Next/previous line
- *Enter*: Execute command

Here are few keyboard shortcuts for Atom text editor:

- *Ctrl + B*: Browse list of open files
- *Ctrl +Alt + R*: Reload Atom
- *Ctrl +Shift + L*: Change syntax highlighting
- *Alt +Shift + S*: Show available code snippets
- *Ctrl +Shift + M*: Markdown preview
- *Ctrl +Alt + I*: Toggle Developer Tools
- *Ctrl + N*: New file
- *Ctrl +Shift + N*: New Window
- *Ctrl + P*: Open file (type the name to perform a search)
- *Ctrl + O*: Open file
- *Ctrl +Shift + O*: Open folder
- *Ctrl + S*: Save
- *Ctrl +Shift + S*: Save as
- *Ctrl + W*: Close tab
- *Ctrl +Shift + W*: Close window
- *Ctrl + G*: Go to line
- *Ctrl + L*: Select line
- *Ctrl +Shift + D*: Duplicate line
- *Ctrl +Shift + K*: Delete line
- *Ctrl + Up/Down*: Move line up/down
- *Ctrl + /*: Toggle comment line
- *Ctrl + Enter*: New line below
- *Ctrl + [/]*: Indent/unindent selected lines
- *Ctrl + J*: Join lines
- *Ctrl + Alt + .*: Complete bracket
- *Ctrl + M*: Go to matching bracket
- *Ctrl + Alt + M*: Select code inside matching brackets

- *Ctrl + Alt + /*: Fold/unfold code
- *Ctrl + Alt + F*: Fold selected code
- *Ctrl + Alt + [/]*: Fold/unfold all code
- *Ctrl + F*: Find in current file
- *Ctrl + Shift + F*: Find in project
- *F3*: Find next
- *Shift + F3*: Find previous
- *Ctrl + Enter*: Replace all
- *Ctrl + Alt + /*: Use Regex in search
- *Ctrl + Shift + =/-*: Increase/decrease text size
- *Ctrl + 0* (zero): Reset text size
- *F11*: Toggle fullscreen

Why do we use Chrome Developer Tools?

The following points the use of Chrome Developer Tools:

- Easy to see the errors
- Easy to edit/debug codes using the line numbers
- Real-time output (No need to refresh the page)

Why do we use Atom as the text editor?

The following points the use of Atom as the text editor:

- Zero-compromise combination of hackability and usability
- An open source text editor
- Every Atom window is essentially a locally-rendered web page

Exercise

To enhance your knowledge of JavaScript, write a program that will print your name.

Summary

In this chapter, we saw how to download Google Chrome and Atom, and install them.

You learned how to write your first code using Chrome Developer Tools (**Console**). You have also learned a few keyboard shortcuts for Chrome Developer Tools and Atom text editor.

You also learned what JavaScript is, why learning JavaScript is important, and how JavaScript is different from other languages.

We can now jump in the world of JavaScript.

Your journey begins from *Chapter 2, Solving Problems Using JavaScript*.

2
Solving Problems Using JavaScript

You have learned how to print something using JavaScript on console in the previous chapter. Now, let's see the fundamentals behind JavaScript syntax, variables, arithmetic operators, and comments.

In the computer world, there is nothing but data. You can read, modify, and create new data; however, anything that isn't data simply does not exist. In JavaScript, we need to handle data to develop a website.

To understand the basic syntax of JavaScript, first of all you need to know that JavaScript is *case sensitive*. You cannot interchange lower case and upper case letters in JavaScript. Therefore, when dealing with the JavaScript syntax, you need to remember that writing the code is not the only important task, you must also watch the syntax whether it's written correctly.

Let me show you an example. In the previous chapter, you have successfully printed **Hello World** on your browser using the `document.write();` syntax.

What would happen if you wrote `Document.write("Hello World");`? Yes! It won't run successfully. You will get an error message. This kind of errors is known as **Uncaught SyntaxError**.

A JavaScript statement is typically written on one line. You may finish your statement with a semicolon or not. It is not mandatory to end a statement with a semicolon. However, it is a good practice to add a semicolon after each statement.

Let's consider the following example:

```
document.write("Hello");
document.write("World");
document.write("!");
```

Its output will be as follows:

HelloWorld!	Elements Console Sources Network Timeline Profiles Resources Audits
	⊘ ▽ <top frame> ▼ ☐ Preserve log ☑ Show all messages
	> document.write("Hello");
	document.write("World");
	document.write("!");
	← undefined
	> |

 JavaScript keywords (such as for, while, if, switch, case, and so on) are always in lowercase. The build-in objects (such as Date, Math, Number, and so on) start with uppercase.

Variables

We already know that the computer world has nothing but data.

There are different types of data (we call them *data types*), as follows:

- Your name is a kind of data
- Your age is data
- Your grade is also data

Yet, they all are different. What is the difference between them? Your name only contains a group of *characters* or, as some people also call it, **string**. Your age is an **integer** type data. Your grade is a **float** type data. The wonderful thing in JavaScript is that you do not have to specify the data type before writing a *variable's* name.

 JavaScript allows working with three data types. Strings (for example, "This is an example of string"), numbers (for example, 2015, 3.1415, and so on), and Boolean (for example, true or false).

Did we discuss *variables*? Well, you already know the data types. You will need *something* to store your data. This *something* is called *variable*. In JavaScript, we use var before the variable names. Remember that var starts with small letter.

Let's consider the following example:

```
var x;
var y;
var sum;
var name;
```

Let's say that we have 14 apples and 6 oranges. To store them in variables we will use the following:

```
var apples = 14;
var oranges = 6;
```

The following example is not the same. Can you tell why?

```
var Apples = 14;
var apples = 14;
var APPLES = 14;
var appleS = 14;
```

Yes, JavaScript is case sensitive. All the variables are different here, though the values of the variables are the same.

Now, let's do some coding. Previously, on console, you printed your name as homework. I hope you did it without any trouble. How about we now print your name differently using a variable? Assume that your name is `Sherlock Holmes`. What kind of data is it?

You are right, it is *string* type. Usually for string type data, we put the string between two quotes.

Let's consider the following example:

```
var name = "Sherlock Holmes";
var occupation = "Detective"
```

To print them using console, you need to type each statement and press *Enter*. Take a look at the following image:

 Do not copy and paste the codes on the console. You might get a syntax error.

You will see an extra line appearing after you hit *Enter*, stating `undefined`. Don't worry about this for now. It just returned a console log.

You stored the `Sherlock Holmes` string on the `name` variable and you stored `Detective` on `occupation`. Every time you access `name` or `occupation`, you can access the stated strings.

Consider that you want to print **Sherlock Holmes** on your screen. Just type the following:

```
document.write(name);
```

After typing, hit *Enter*. You will see **Sherlock Holmes** is printed on the screen, as follows:

Type `document.write(occupation);` and hit *Enter*, as shown in the following screenshot:

You may be wondering why is there no space between **Sherlock Holmes** and **Detective**. As, on the console, the history is not automatically removed from the web page on the left-hand side and after you hit *Enter* for your second output (`occupation`), the string places itself right after the previous string. This will always happen, unless you clear your console using the *Ctrl + L* keyboard shortcut and reload the web page pressing the key *F5*.

 Your stored variables will also be erased from the memory when you reload the web page. Don't worry, you will be taught how to use your variables storing on a file in the next chapter.

If you want to join two (or multiple) variables, you add a plus sign (+) between the two variables, as follows:

```
document.write(name+occupation);
document.write(occupation+name);
```

Can you tell me what will be output of these commands?

Yes, you are right. The output will be as follows:

Sherlock HolmesDetective

DetectiveSherlock Holmes

 Your output might be in one line on the web page. If you want to split the lines, add a `<br>` HTML tag. The simplest way to add this is to type `document.write("<br>");` and hit *Enter*. Your next output will be in a new line.

If you want to add any string (for example, a space) between the two strings other than any variables, just type the following:

```
document.write(name+" "+occupation);
```

The output will be as follows:

Sherlock Holmes Detective

What will happen when you type the following code and hit *Enter*?

```
document.write("My name is "+name+" and I am a "+occupation);
```

Yes! You are absolutely right. The output will be as shown in the following:

My name is Sherlock Holmes and I am a Detective

Now, add another variable on the console. Consider that `Sherlock Holmes` is 24 years old. Do you remember what kind of data age is?

Yes, it is an integer type of number. Therefore, type the following code and hit *Enter*:

```
var age = 24;
```

You have the following three variables now:

- Name
- Occupation
- Age

Let's print the following output on the web page:

My name is Sherlock Holmes, I'm 24 years old and I am a Detective

What will our code be on the console?

The code is as follows:

```
document.write("My name is "+name+", I\'m "+age+" years old and I
   am a "+occupation);
```

The output can be seen as follows:

mage_ref id="1" />

Printing quotations/inverted commas

If you want to print **Shakespeare said, "To be, or not to be: that is the question!"** using the `document.write();` syntax, you will probably type the following code:

```
document.write("Shakespeare said, "To be, or not to be:
   that is the question!"");
```

However, this will give you an error known as **SyntaxError**. To get rid of this error, you need to use a backward slash (\) before the two inverted commas. The correct code will be as follows:

```
document.write("Shakespeare said, \"To be, or not to
   be: that is the question!\"");
```

The output will be as shown in the following:

Shakespeare said, "To be, or not to be: that is the question!"

The same rule applies for single inverted comma (').

Here is a quick exercise for you:

1. Suppose `Tom` has a cat (`Lucy`). The cat, `Lucy`, is `2.4` years old. Store the name, cat's name, and its age on three different variables and print the following output using console:

   Tom's cat Lucy is 2.4 years old.

2. Assume that you bought `4` pounds of apples. Each pound costs you `$1.2`. Store the price and quantity of apples on two different variables and print the following output using console:

   I bought 4 pounds of apples. I had to pay $1.2 for each pound.

Comments

Suppose you have done a lot of coding and some logical operations, and used a number of variables on JavaScript, and you want me to help you with the code if any errors occur. When you send me the code, I will not know what you have typed unless I have a clear knowledge of JavaScript or you have commented on the important lines.

A comment is basically a line of text or code that your browser ignores while running. You can compare comments to sticky notes or reminder.

Let's consider the following example:

```
Var name = "Sherlock Holmes"; // This is a string
Var occupation = "Detective"; // This variable stores information
Var age = 14; // This is an integer type of data.
```

How do you make multiline comments? You mention the comment in the following manner:

```
/*
   This is a multiline comment.
   The browser will ignore this.
   You can type any important information on your comment.
*/
```

Your multiline comment should be between /* and */, as shown in the following screenshot:

Arithmetic operators

In JavaScript, like other programming languages, we can do some arithmetic operations. In your school, you might have already learned how to add two numbers, subtract one number from another number, multiply two numbers, and divide a number with another. You can do all these things in JavaScript with the help of a few lines of code.

In JavaScript, we use the following arithmetic symbols for the operations:

Operator	Description
+	To add
-	To subtract
*	To multiply
/	To divide
%	To find the reminder (called modulus operator)

Addition

Suppose you have two variables, x and y, with the values 3 and 4, respectively. What should we do on the console to store the values on the variables?

Yes, we do the following:

```
var x = 3; // 3 is stored on variable x
var y = 4; // 4 is stored on variable y
```

Then, press *Enter*.

Take another variable that will hold the summation of x and y, as follows:

```
var z = x+y; // This syntax stores the sum of x and y on z
```

Can you tell me what will happen when we print z?

```
document.write(z);
```

Yes, you are correct, this will print **7**, as shown in the following screenshot:

Subtraction

To subtract a number from another, you need to put a minus sign (-) between them.

Let's consider the following example:

```
var x = 9; // 9 is assigned to the variable x.
var y = 3; // 3 is assigned to the variable y.
var z = x - y ; // This syntax subtracts y from x and stores on z.
document.write(z); // Prints the value of z.
```

The output of this code is **6**, as shown in the following screenshot:

Multiplication

To multiply two numbers or variables that have integer or float type of data stored on them, you just put an asterisk (*) between the variables or numbers.

Let's take a look at the following example:

```
var x = 6; // 6 is assigned to the variable x.
var y = 2; // 2 is assigned to the variable y.
var z = x * y; // For two numbers you can type z = 6 * 2 ;
document.write(z); // Prints the value of z
```

The output of this code is **12**, as shown in the following screenshot:

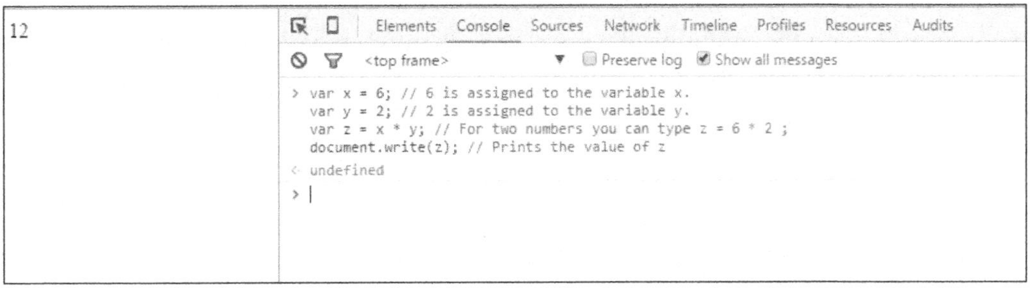

Division

To divide a number with another, you need to put a forward slash (/) between the numbers.

Let's take a look at the following example:

```
var x = 14; // assigns 14 on variable x.
var y = 2; // assigns 2 on variable y.
var z = x / y; // divides x with y and stores the value on z.
document.write(z); // prints the value of z.
```

The output of this code is **7**, as shown in the following screenshot:

```
7                          Q 🔲   Elements  Network  Sources  Timeline  Profiles  Console  »

                           ⊘ ▽  <top frame>              ▼  ☐ Preserve log  ☑ Show all messages

                           > var x = 14; // assigns 14 on variable x.
                             var y = 2; // assigns 2 on variable y.
                             var z = x / y; // divides x with y and stores the value on z.
                             document.write(z); // prints the value of z
                           ⬅ undefined
                           >
```

Modulus

If you want to find the modulus of a number with another, you need to put a percentage sign (%) between the numbers.

Let's consider the following example:

```
var x = 34; // assigns 34 on the variable x.
var y = 3; // assigns 3 on the variable y.
var z = x % y ; // divides x with y and returns the reminder and
    stores on the variable z
document.write(z);
```

The output of this code is **1**, as shown in the following screenshot:

```
1                          Q 🔲   Elements  Network  Sources  Timeline  Profiles  Console  »      >_  ⚙ 🖵

                           ⊘ ▽  <top frame>              ▼  ☐ Preserve log  ☑ Show all messages

                           > var x = 34; // assigns 34 on the variable x.
                               var y = 3; // assigns 3 on the variable y.
                               var z = x % y ; // divides x with y and returns the reminder and stores on the
                             variable z
                               document.write(z);
                           ⬅ undefined
                           > |
```

What does modulus (%) operator do?

Well, from your math class, you have already learned how to divide one number with another. Say, you divide 10 by 2. The result will be 5, which is an integer type of number. However, what will happen if you divide 10 by 3? The answer will not be an integer. The value is 3.333333333333. You can also say that the answer is 3 and the remainder is 1. Consider the following:

```
10 = 9 + 1;
```
That is, `(9+1)/3`
```
= 9/3+1/3
= 3 + 1/3;
```
Therefore, the remainder is 1. What modulus does is that it finds out the remainder and returns it. Therefore, `10%3 = 1`.

Now, let's summarize all the arithmetic operators that we learned so far in one single code.

Can you tell me the output of the following lines?

```
var x = 5 ;
var y = 4 ;
var sum = x + y ;
var sub = x - y ;
var mul = x * y ;
var div = x / y ;
var mod = x % y ;
document.write("The summation of x and y is "+ sum + "<br>") ;
document.write("The subtraction of x and y is " + sub + "<br>") ;
document.write("The multiplication of x and y is " + mul +
   "<br>");
document.write("The division of x and y is " + div + "<br>") ;
document.write("The modulus of x and y is " + mod + "<br>") ;
```

You will get the following output:

The summation of x and y is 9

The subtraction of x and y is 1

The multiplication of x and y is 20

The division of x and y is 1.25

The modulus of x and y is 1

This output can be seen in the following screenshot:

```
The summation of x and y is 9
The subtraction of x and y is 1
The multiplication of x and y is 20
The division of x and y is 1.25
The modulus of x and y is 1
```

I guess you nailed it. Now, let's explain them in the following:

- We assigned 5 and 4 to x and y, respectively
- We assigned the summation of x and y to the `sum` variable, the subtraction of x and y to the `sub` variable, the multiplication of x and y to the `mul` variable, the division of x and y to the `div` variable, and the modulus of x and y to the `mod` variable
- Then, we printed them using the `document.write();` syntax
- We used a `<br>` HTML tag to separate the output of each line

Consider the following example:

John has 56 pens. He wants to arrange them in seven rows. Each line will have an equal number of pens. Write a code that will print the number of pens in each row.

(Hint: take two variables for the number of pens and number of rows, divide the number of pens with the number of rows and store the value in a new variable.)

The sample output is as follows:

John will have to place XX pens on each line. // XX is the number of pens

More operators and operations

JavaScript has more operators other than those stated earlier. Let's go little bit deeper.

Increment or decrement operators

If you have an integer and you want to increment it by 1 or any number, you can type the following:

```
var x = 4; // assigns 4 on the variable x.
x = x + 1;
/* since x=4, and you are adding 1 with x, so the final value is
   4 + 1 = 5, and 5 is stored on the same variable x. */
```

You can also increment your variable by 1, typing the following:

```
var x = 4; // assigns 4 on the variable x.
x++; // This is similar to x = x + 1.
```

What will you do if you want to increment your variable by more than 1? Well, you can follow this:

```
var x = 4; // assigns 4 on the variable x.
x = x + 3; // Say, you want to increment x by 3.
/* since x = 4, and you are adding 3 with x, so the final value is
   4 + 3 = 7, and 7 is stored on the same variable x. */
```

You can increment your variable by typing the following as well:

```
var x = 4; // assigns 4 on the variable x.
x += 3; // This is similar to x = x + 3.
```

 Remember that you should not place a space between an operator (for example +, -, *, /, and so on) and equal sign (=).

The output will look similar to the following screenshot on the console:

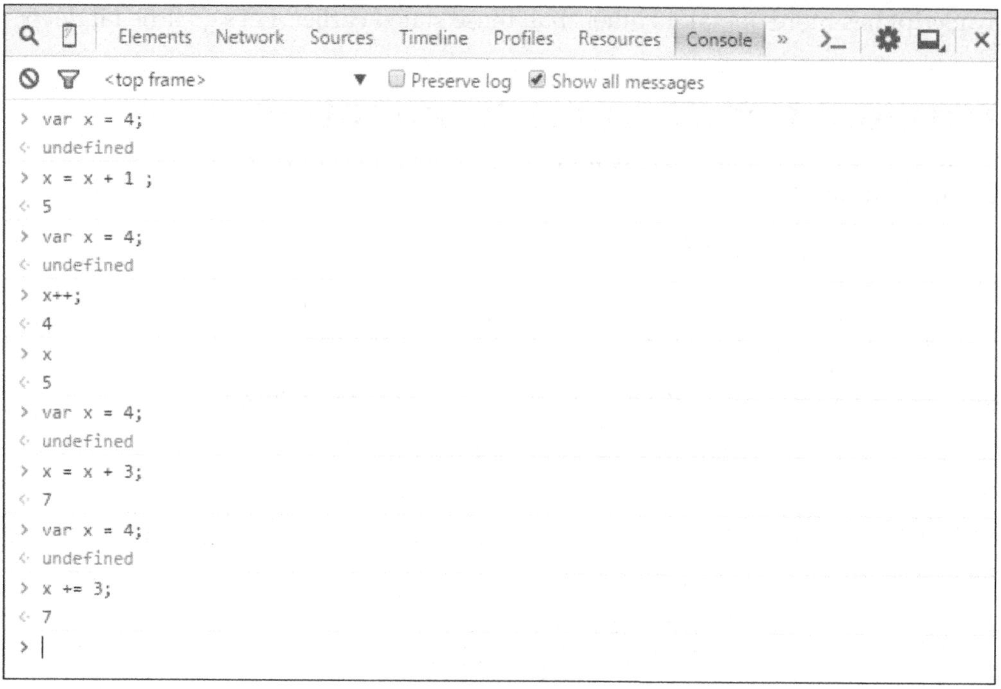

What about the decrement operator? Yes, you are absolutely right. Decrement operations are same as the increment operations. The only thing that changes is the sign. Your addition (+) operator will be replaced by the subtraction operator (-). Let's take a look at an example:

```
var x = 9; // assigns 9 on the variable x.
x = x - 1;
/* since x = 9, and you are subtracting 1 from x, so the final
   value is 9 - 1 = 8, and 8 is stored on the same variable x. */
```

You can also decrement your variable by 1 typing the following:

```
var x = 9; // assigns 9 on the variable x.
x--; // This is similar to x = x - 1.
```

What will you do if you want to decrement your variable by more than 1? Well, you can follow this:

```
var x = 9; // assigns 9 on the variable x.
x = x - 4; // Say, you want to decrement x by 4.
/* since x = 9, and you are subtracting 4 from x, so the final
   value is 9 - 4 = 5, and 5 is stored on the same variable x. */
```

You can also decrement your variable by typing the following:

```
var x = 9; // assigns 9 on the variable x.
x -= 4; // This is similar to x = x - 4.
```

The output of these codes can be seen in the following screenshot:

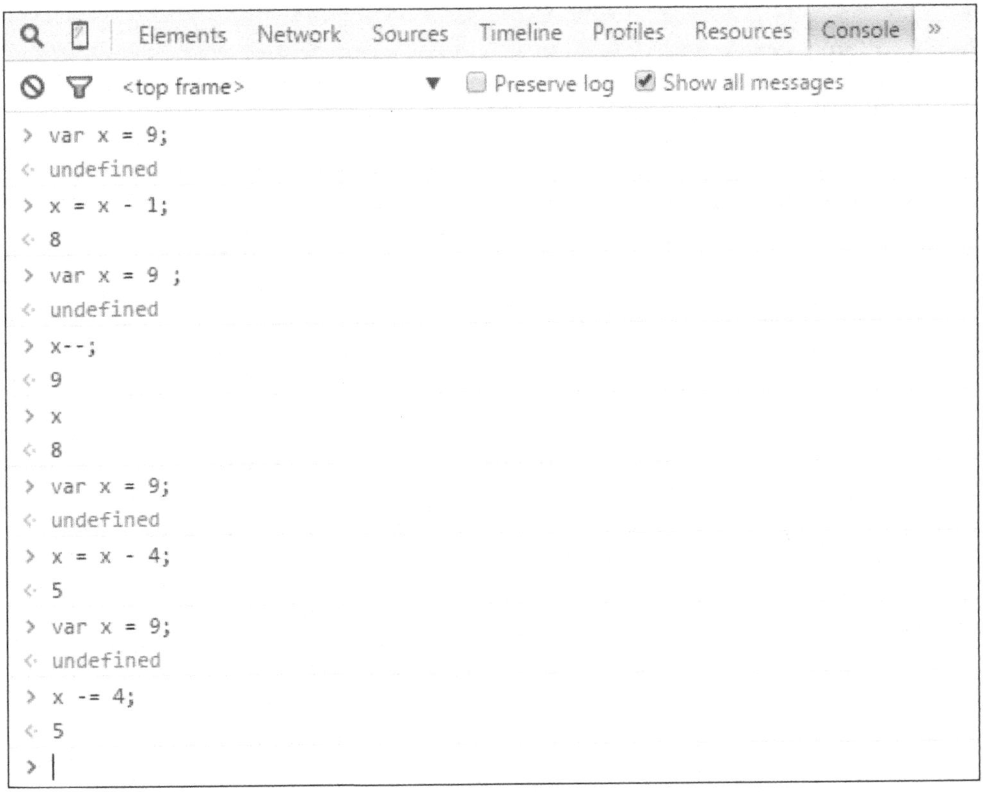

These type of operations are very important for logical operations in JavaScript. You will learn about their uses in *Chapter 4, Diving a Bit Deeper*.

Assignment operators

An assignment operator assigns a value to an operator. I believe that you already know about assignment operators, don't you? Well, you use an equal sign (=) between a variable and its value. By doing this, you assigned the value to the variable.

Let's take a look at the following example:

```
var name = "Sherlock Holmes"
```

The `Sherlock Holmes` string is assigned to the `name` variable. You have already learned about increment and decrement operators. Can you tell me what will the output of the following codes be?

```
var x = 3;
x *= 2;
document.write(x);
```

The output will be **6**.

Do you remember why this has happened?

The `x *= 2;` equation is similar to `x = x * 2;` as x is equal to 3, and later it is multiplied by 2. The final number (3 x 2 = 6) is assigned to the same x variable. That's why we got the following output:

6	Q ☐ Elements Network Sources Timeline Profiles Resources │ Console »
	⊘ ▽ \<top frame\> ▼ ☐ Preserve log ☑ Show all messages
	> var x = 3;
	x *= 2;
	document.write(x);
	← undefined
	> │

Let's perform the following exercise:

What is the output of the following code?

```
var w = 32;
var x = 12;
var y = 9;
var z = 5;
w++;
w--;
x*2;
y = x;
y--;
z%2;
document.write(" w = "+w+ ", x = "+x+ ", y =   "+ y+", z =   "+z  );
```

We will get the following output:

w = 32, x = 12, y = 11, z = 5

This output can be seen in the following screenshot:

```
w = 32, x = 12, y = 11, z = 5
```

```
              Elements   Console   Sources   Network   Timeline   Profiles   Resources   Audits
    ⃠  ▽  <top frame>                 ▼   ☐ Preserve log  ☑ Show all messages
> var w = 32;
  var x = 12;
  var y = 9;
  var z = 5 ;
  w++ ;
  w-- ;
  x*2 ;
  y = x ;
  y-- ;
  z%2 ;
  document.write(" w = "+w+ ", x = "+x+ ", y =  "+ y+", z =  "+z  ) ;
⟵ undefined
> |
```

JavaScript comparison and logical operators

If you want to do something logical and compare two numbers or variables in JavaScript, you need to use a few logical operators. The following are a few examples of the comparison operators:

Operator	Description
==	Equal to
!=	Not equal to
>	Greater than
<	Less than
=>	Equal to or greater than
<=	Less than or equal to

The following are a few examples that use these operators:

You will learn more about the use of these operators in the following chapters.

Let's discuss a few bitwise logical operators and bitwise operators:

Operators	Description
&&	This means the AND operator. To check whether two or more statements are true, we use this.
||	This means the OR operator. To check whether any of the statement is true, we use this.
~	This means the NOT operator.
^	This means the XOR operator.
>>	This means the Right Shift operator.
<<	This means the Left Shift operator.

They might be hard for you to learn right now. Don't worry, you don't have to use them now. We will use them in *Chapter 4, Diving a Bit Deeper*.

Summary

In this chapter, you learned about the JavaScript syntax. We discussed the JavaScript variables and how to assign a value to a variable. You learned how to comment on the code. You now know why commenting is important. You finally learned an important topic: operators and operations. JavaScript, without using operators and logical functions, will not be so rich nowadays. Therefore, learning about the logical operations is the key to gain good knowledge of JavaScript.

I would like to suggest you to practice all the code in this chapter at home. You just type them on the console, avoid copying and pasting the codes. This will hamper with your learning. As a programmer must have a good typing speed, copying and pasting the codes will not improve this skill. You may face problems in typing codes; however, you will learn.

You can solve any arithmetic problem using JavaScript. You can also check whether your logic is true or false on console. If you can do this, we can move on to the next chapter, *Chapter 3*, *Introducing HTML and CSS*, where you will learn about HTML, CSS, and so on.

3

Introducing HTML and CSS

You have already learned about JavaScript syntax, arithmetic operators, and comment in the previous chapter. We used console for these purposes. Now, how about you learn something interesting, which will pave the way for you to be a good JavaScript programmer? In this chapter, we are going to study about the **HyperText Markup Language** (**HTML**) syntax, **Cascading Style Sheets** (**CSS**) syntax, and how to use JavaScript in an HTML page.

HTML is the source code of a web page. All the web pages that you load on your web browser are built with HTML. Go to any website (for example, `https://www.google.com`) and press *Ctrl + U* (on Mac, click *command + U*) on your keyboard, you will get the web page's source code. This works on all modern web browsers, such as Firefox, Google Chrome, UC, and so on.

The entire code that you will see is in HTML. You may also find a few lines with JavaScript. Therefore, in order to understand the structure of a web page (the code behind the page), you need to know about HTML. This is one of the easiest languages on the web.

HTML

HTML is a markup language. What does it mean? Well, a markup language processes and presents texts using specific codes for formatting, styling, and layout design. There are a lot of markup languages (for example, **Business Narrative Markup Language** (**BNML**), **ColdFusion Markup Language** (**CFML**), **Opera Binary Markup Language** (**OBML**), **Systems Biology Markup Language** (**SBML**), **Virtual Human Markup Language** (**VHML**), and so on); however, in modern web, we use HTML. HTML is based on **Standard Generalized Markup Language** (**SGML**). SGML was basically used to design document papers.

There are a number of HTML versions. HTML 5 is the latest version. Throughout this book, we will use the latest version of HTML.

Before you start learning HTML, let me ask you to think of your favorite website. What does the website contain? A few web pages? You may see some text, few images, one or two text fields, buttons, and some more elements on each of the web pages. Each of these elements are formatted by HTML.

Let me introduce you to a web page. On your Internet browser, go to `https://www.google.com`. You will see a page as shown in the following image:

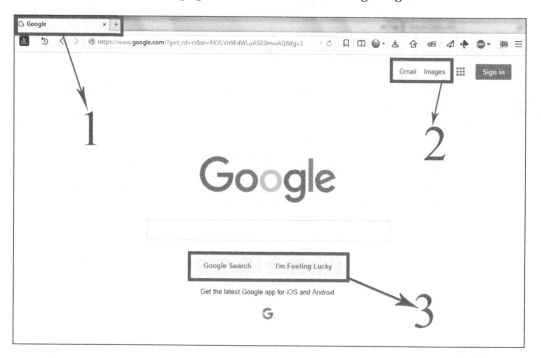

The first thing you will see on the top of your browser is the title of the webpage. Let's observe the page that we just loaded:

- Here, the marked box, **1**, is the title of the web page that we loaded.
- The second box, **2**, indicates some links or text.
- The word **Google** in the middle of the page is an image.
- The third box, **3**, consists of two buttons.
- Can you tell me what **Sign in** on the right-hand top of the page is? Yes, it is a button.

Let's demonstrate the basic structure of HTML. The term *tag* will be used frequently to demonstrate the structure.

An HTML tag is nothing but a few predefined words between the less than sign (<) and greater than sign (>). Therefore, the structure of a tag is <WORD>, where WORD is the predefined text that is recognized by the Internet browsers. This type of tag is called open tag. There is another type of tag that is known as close tag. The structure of a close tag is similar to </WORD>. You just have to put a forward slash after the less than sign.

After this section, you will be able to make your own web page with some text using HTML. The structure of an HTML page is similar to the following image. This image has eight tags. Let's introduce all these tags with their activities, as shown in the following:

```
1    <html>------------------(1)
2
3    <head>------------------(2)
4    <title>-----------------(3)
5
6    </title>----------------(4)
7    </head>-----------------(5)
8
9
10   <body>------------------(6)
11
12
13   </body>-----------------(7)
14
15   </html>-----------------(8)
```

- **1**: The tag <html> is an open tag and it closes at line **15** with the </html> tag.
  - These tags tell your Internet browser that all the texts and scripts in these two tags are HTML documents.

- **2**: This is the <head> tag, which is an open tag and closes at line **7** with the </head> tag.
  - These tags contain the title, script, style, and metadata of a web page.

- **3**: This is the `<title>` tag, and closes at line **4** with the `</title>` tag.
  - ◦ This tag contains the title of the web page. The previous image had the title **Google**. To see this on the web browser, you need to type the following:
    ```
    <title> Google </title>
    ```

- **4**: This is the close tag of the `<title>` tag.

- **5**: This is the closing tag of the `<head>` tag.

- **6**: This is the `<body>` tag, and closes at line **13** with the `</body>` tag.

  Everything you can see on a webpage is written between these two tags. Every element, image, link and so on are formatted here. To see This is a web page. on your browser, you need to type the following:
  ```
  <body>
  This is a web page.
  </body>
  ```

- **7**: The `</body>` tag closes here.

- **8**: The `</html>` tag is closes here.

Your first webpage

You just learned the eight basic tags of an HTML page. You can now make your own web page. How? Why not try with me?

1. Open your text editor (You have already installed Atom in *Chapter 1, Exploring JavaScript in the Console* of this book).

2. Press *Ctrl + N*, which will open a new `untitled` file as shown in the following image:

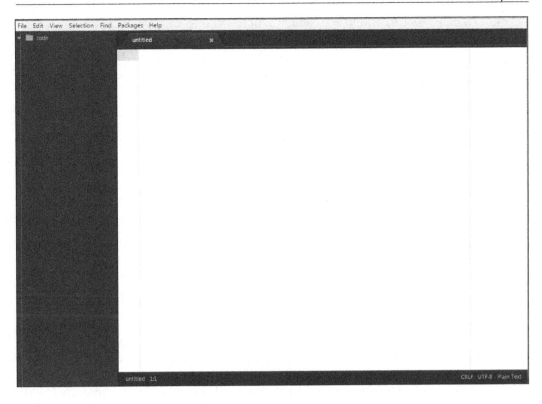

3. Type the following HTML codes on a blank page:

```
<html>
  <head>
    <title>
      My Webpage!
    </title>
  </head>
  <body>
    This is my webpage :)
  </body>
</html>
```

4. Then, press *Ctrl + Shift + S*, which will tell you to save your code somewhere on your computer:

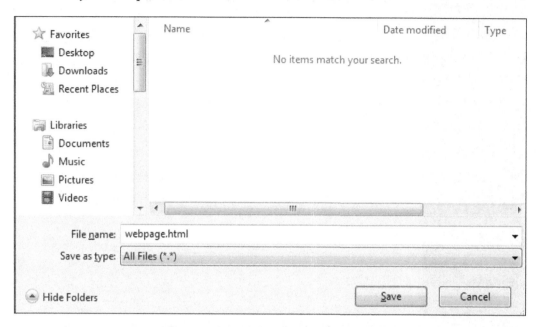

5. Type a suitable name on the **File name:** field. I would like to name my HTML file webpage, therefore, I typed webpage.html. You may be wondering why I added an extension (.html).

As this is an HTML document, you need to add .html or .htm after the name that you give your webpage. The .htm extension is an old form of .html. It was limited to keep the file extension in three characters, therefore, people used .htm instead of .html. You can also use .htm.

6. Press the **Save** button. This will create an HTML document on your computer. Go to the directory, where you just have saved your HTML file.

Remember that you can give your web page any name. However, this name will not be visible on your browser. It is not the title of your web page. It is good practice not to keep a blank space in your webpage's name. For example, you want to name your HTML file This is my first webpage.html. Your computer will face no problem showing the result on the Internet browsers; however, when your website will be on a server, this name might face a problem. Therefore, I would suggest you to keep an underscore (_) where you need to add a space, such as This_is_my_first_webpage.html.

7. You will find a file similar to the following image:

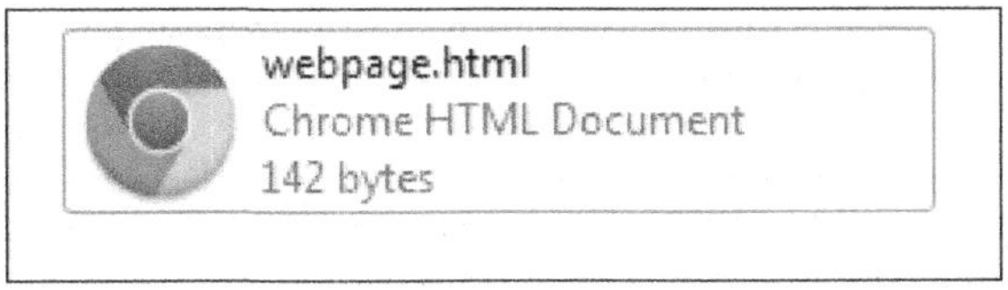
webpage.html
Chrome HTML Document
142 bytes

8. Now, double-click on the file. You will see your first web page on the Internet browser!

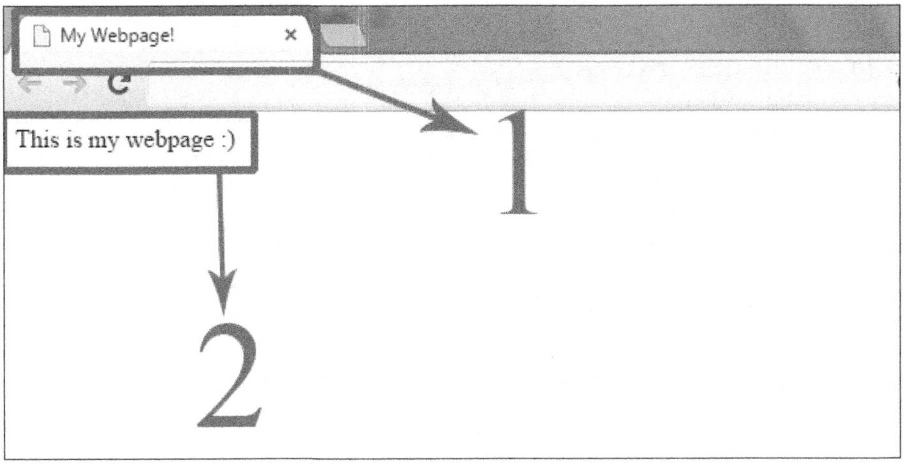
My Webpage!
This is my webpage :)
1
2

You typed `My Webpage!` between the `<title>` and `</title>` tags, which is why your browser shows this in the first selection box, **1**. You typed `This is my webpage :)` between the `<body>` and `</body>` tags. Therefore, you can see the text on your browser in the second selection box, **2**.

Congratulations! You created your first web page!

> You can edit your codes and other texts of the `webpage.html` file by right-clicking on the file and select **Open with Atom**. You must save (*Ctrl* + *S*) your codes and text before reopening the file in your browser.

More HTML tags

There are a number of HTML tags to format text and objects of your web page. How about we study a few of them now?

Description	Syntax with example	Result on browser
Bold Text	`<b> This is bold </b>`	**This is bold**
Italic Text	`<i> This is italic </i>`	*This is italic*
Underlined Text	`<u> Underline Text </u>`	<u>Underline Text</u>
Deleted Text	`<del> Delete me </del>`	~~Delete me~~
Subscript Text	`CO<sub>2</sub>`	CO_2
Superscript	`3x10<sup>8</sup>`	$3x10^8$
Largest headline	`<h1> Hi Kids! </h1>`	**Hi Kids!**
Smallest headline	`<h6> Hi Kids </h6>`	**Hi Kids**
Paragraph Text	`<p>This is a paragraph </p>`	This is a paragraph
Break Tag	`This  is  a break;`	This is a break;

There are six headline tags (`<h1>` to `<h6>`). You can add more than one tag for a text if required. For example: `<b><i><u> JavaScript </b></i></u>` will have the following output: *JavaScript* . There is no specific order in which you should close the tags. The best practice is to follow the sequence of open tags.

Coloring HTML text

To color an HTML text, we can type the following:

```
<font color = "Green"> I am green </font>
```

You can type any standard color name between the two inverted commas (" "). You can also use hex color code, as follows:

```
<font color = "#32CD32"> I am green </font>
```

Here, 32CD32 is the hex code of green. Look at the following image. The left-hand side is the code, where we used both color name and hex code. On the right-hand side, we got the output of our browser:

```
<html>
    <head>
        <title>
        My Webpage!
        </title>
    </head>
    <body>
        <font color = "Green">This is green</font><br>
        <font color = "#32CD32"> This is also green </font>
    </body>
</html>
```

My Webpage!   ×

← → C

This is green
This is also green

A hex color code consists of six digits (it is a hexadecimal number). It starts with a pound sign or hash sign (#) and we place the six digit hexadecimal number after it. The hexadecimal number represents red, blue, and green colors' amount. Each two digits represents 00 to FF (hexadecimal number). In the example, we used #32CD32 for green. 32, CD, and 32 are the amount of red, blue, and green; respectively; in hexadecimal.

If you don't know what a hexadecimal number is, remember that we use decimal number where 10 digits (0, 1, 2, 3, 4, 5, 6, 7, 8, and 9) are used. However, in hexadecimal numbers, we use 16 digits (0, 1, 2, 3, 4, 5, 6, 7, 8, 9, A, B, C, D, E, and F).

I would recommend you to use this website (http://html-color-codes.info/) to get your favorite color's hex code without thinking about the hex code.

Linking HTML text

To hyperlink a text, we use an anchor tag as follows:

```
<a href = "http://www.google.com"> Go to Google </a>
```

The output of this code will be a link. If you click on the link, it will send you to the URL that we used between the inverted commas (here, http://www.google.com).

If you want to open your link in a new tab of your browser, you need to add a target as shown in the following:

```
<a href = "http://google.com" target = "_blank" > Go to Google
</a>
```

Here, `target = "_blank"` is an attribute that tells your browser to open the link in a new tab. There are few more attributes. You can try them at home and let us know what you see on your browser.

The other attributes are `_parent`, `_self`, and `_top`. The following image has the code that has the `_blank` attribute. It opens `http://google.com` in a new tab. I would suggest you to find what the other attributes do:

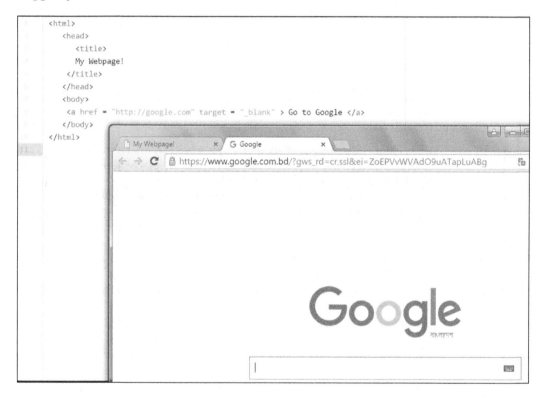

Inserting an image

Inserting an image on an HTML document is super easy. You just have to find the image file extensions. The tag that we use to insert an image is as shown in the following:

```
<img src = "Image_name.extension">
```

The `src` attribute is the source of your image. If your image is placed on the same directory of the HTML file, you don't have to write the whole file source. Throughout this book, we will keep our image files on the same directory, where we save our HTML files.

Let's say that I have an image in the same folder where I saved the HTML document. The name of the image is `physics` and its extension is `.png`. Now, to add this on the HTML document, I need to add the following code:

```
<img src= "physics.png">
```

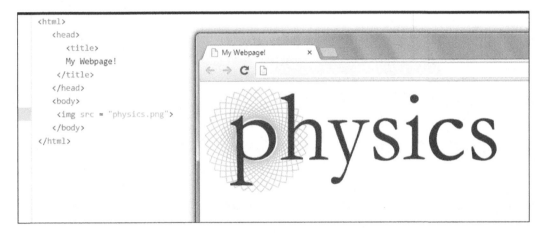

 We use three types of images on an HTML document. **Portable Network Graphics (PNG)**, **Graphics Interchange Format (GIF)** and **Joint Photographic Experts Group (JPG** or **JPEG)**. To find your image's extension, right-click on your image, go to **Properties**, and then, click on the **Details** tab to scroll down until you find the **Name** field. You will find the image name with the extension. The procedure might be different on your machine, depending on your operating system.

If you want to set the height and width of the image, you need to use two attributes, as shown in the following:

```
< img src = "physics.png" width="100" height="40">
```

Here, `100` and `40` are the pixel of the image. In the previous versions of HTML, it was defined as pixels or percentage.

 A pixel is the smallest unit of an image. Using percentage (%) is better if you want to see the same ratio of the image on different screen sizes, otherwise, you can use the pixel (px) unit.

The output will look similar to the following:

```
<html>
    <head>
        <title>
        My Webpage!
        </title>
    </head>
    <body>
        <img src = "physics.png" width="100" height="40">
    </body>
</html>
```

There are more HTML tags; however, we have covered most of the tags that we use to build a web page. Can you imagine the output of the following codes?

```
<html>
    <head>
        <title>
            Example
        </title>
    </head>
    <body>
        <h1> This is a headline </h1>
        <h2> This is a headline </h2>
```

```
    <h3> This is a headline </h3>
    <h4> This is a headline </h4>
    <h5> This is a headline </h5>
    <h6> This is a headline </h6>
    <b>This is a bold text</b>. But <i>This is an italic text</i>.
      We can <u> underline</u> our text. <a href =
      "http://www.google.com">Go to Google </a> <br>
    <font color = "#AA2FF">This is colorful text</font>
    <br>
    <img src="math.png">
  </body>
</html>
```

The output will look similar to the following image:

CSS

If you want to make your web page beautiful, you must know CSS. CSS is a language that allows you to describe your web pages, color your texts, change the font of the text, and modify the layout of the web page.

There are two parts of a CSS syntax:

- Selector
- Decorator

Before proceeding with learning CSS, you need to introduce yourself with an HTML tag:

```
<style>

</style>
```

This tag should be kept between the `<head></head>` tags. Therefore, the structure of the code will be as shown in the following:

```
<html>
  <head>
    <title>
    </title>
    <style>
      // your codes will be typed here
    </style>
  </head>
  <body>
  </body>
</html>
```

The CSS codes will be written in between the `<style></style>` tags.

To format your text, you need to remember the tag that you used for the text. Consider that you have a text in the `<h1></h1>` tag in the body of the HTML document, as follows:

```
<h1> This is an example of HTML text. </h1>
```

To apply CSS, you need to type the following between the `<style> </style>` tags:

```
<html>
  <head>
    <title>
    </title>
```

```
    <style>
      h1 {
      color:green;
      text-decoration: underline;
      text-align: center;
      }
    </style>
  </head>
  <body>
    <h1>This is an example of HTML text </h1>
  </body>
</html>
```

The output of the code will be as follows:

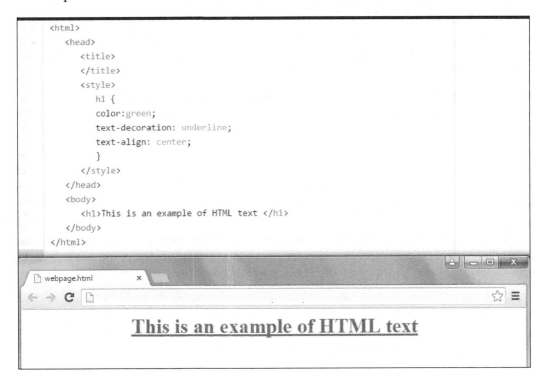

Look at the code carefully. We used the following CSS for the text in the `<h1></h1>` tags:

```
h1 {
color:green;
text-decoration: underline;
text-align: center;
}
```

Here, we used a few CSS syntaxes (`color`, `text-decoration`, and so on). There are a number of CSS syntaxes, also called property (and every property may contain more than one value).

JavaScript on an HTML page

You have already learned how to print something using JavaScript on console. How about we do it on an HTML page? Before doing this, let's introduce an HTML tag, `<script></script>`. Our JavaScript code will be between these tags.

As there are lots of scripting languages, we need to define what kind of language we are using between these tags. Therefore, we type the following:

```
<script type = "text/javascript">
  // Our JavaScript Codes will be here.
</script>
```

The `<script></scripts>` should be in between the `<body></body>` tags.

Let's see an example. In the previous chapter, you learned how to do basic operations using JavaScript on console. Now, we are going to perform a few operations between the `<script></script>` tags in an HTML page. Look at the following code carefully:

```
<html>
  <head>
    <title>
      JavaScript Example
    </title>
  </head>
  <body>
    <script type="text/javascript">
      var x = 34;
      var y = 93;
```

```
        var sum = x+y;
        document.write("The sum of "+x+" and "+y+" is "+sum);
    </script>
  </body>
</html>
```

The output of the code will be as follows:

```
<html>
    <head>
        <title>
            JavaScript Example
        </title>
    </head>
    <body>
        <script type="text/javascript">
            var x = 34;
            var y = 93;
            var sum = x+y;
            document.write("The sum of "+x+" and "+y+" is "+sum);
        </script>
    </body>
</html>
```

JavaScript Example   ✕

← → C

The sum of 34 and 93 is 127

I hope that you could guess the output of the codes by yourself.

Summary

In this chapter, you learned HTML, CSS, and their syntaxes and usages. We also covered how to implement JavaScript on an HTML document. You are now able to build your own web page and make it wonderful using JavaScript. I would suggest you not to skip any part of this chapter in order to have a better understanding of the next chapter, *Chapter 4*, *Diving a Bit Deeper*.

4
Diving a Bit Deeper

In most of the JavaScript programs, which we learned so far, the lines of code were executed in the same order in which they appeared in the program. Each code was executed only once. Thus, the code did not include tests to determine if the conditions were true or false or we did not perform any logical statements.

In this chapter, you are going to learn some logical programming. You will learn about the following topics:

- Loops
- If statement
- Switch case

You already know how to embed JavaScript codes on an HTML document. Before starting this chapter, you will learn a few HTML tags and JavaScript methods. These methods and tags will be used throughout the book.

 In object-oriented programming, we don't directly perform any operations on the data from outside an object; we ask an object to perform the operation by passing one or multiple parameters. This task is called an object's method.

JavaScript methods

In the previous chapters, you learned how to print something using `document.write()`. Now, you will learn something more.

We will check the methods on both console and HTML document, as follows:

- To show an alert or a pop-up box using JavaScript, we use the following method:

```
alert("Hello World");
```

Type this on the console and press *Enter*, you will see a pop-up box saying **Hello World**:

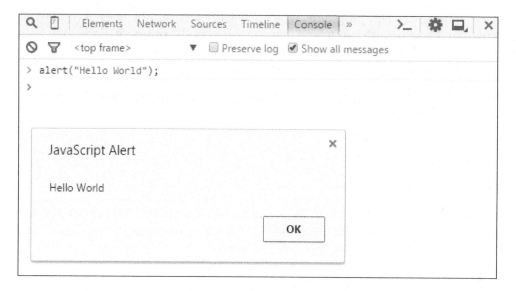

You can write your code to show a pop-up box similar to the following on an HTML document:

```html
<html>
  <head>
    <title>Alert</title>
  </head>
  <body>
    <script type="text/javascript">
      alert("Hello World");

    </script>
  </body>
</html>
```

The output will be as follows:

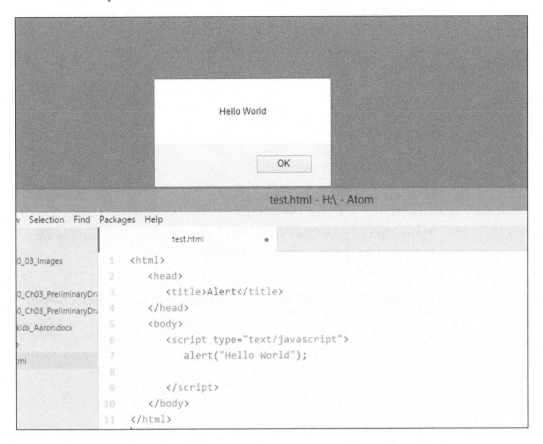

- If you want to take information from users, you need to use a prompt box to do this. Consider the following for example:
    - ○ You want to take input of the username and print it on the main web page.
    - ○ You can do this using the `window.prompt()` method.
    - ○ The structure of `window.prompt()` is similar to the following:
        ```
        window.prompt("What is your name?"); // You can type
            anything between the inverted commas.
        ```
    - ○ Now, you need to store the information on a variable. You already know how to do this from the previous chapters. Type the following and press *Enter*:
        ```
        var name = window.prompt("what is your name?");
        ```

○ After running this code on console, you will be asked to input something on a textbox. After typing your information, you need to press the **OK** button. Your information is now stored in the name variable:

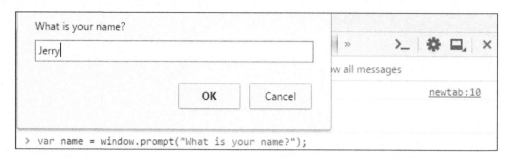

○ If you want to print the variable on your web page, you can use the `document.write();` method, as follows:

```
document.write("Hello "+name+"!");
```

○ The output of these steps can been seen in the following screenshot:

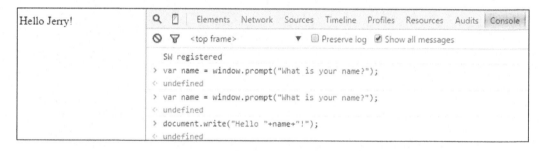

○ The codes on an HTML document will be as shown in the following:

```html
<html>
  <head>
    <title>Prompt</title>
  </head>
  <body>
    <script type="text/javascript">
      var name = window.prompt("What is your name?");
      document.write("Hello "+name+"!");
    </script>
  </body>
</html>
```

HTML buttons and form

In the last chapter, you learned about a few HTML tags. Now, we will study a few tags that will make learning HTML more interesting.

Buttons

If you want to add buttons to your HTML web page, you can use the `<button></button>` tags. The structure of the tags is as follows:

```
<button type="button">Click Here </button>
```

If you want to make your button do something, for example, open an URL; you can consider the following code:

```
<a href="http://google.com/"><button type="button">Click Me
   </button> </a>
```

The output of the code will be as follows:

```
1    <html>
2       <head>
3          <title>Button</title>
4       </head>
5       <body>
6          <a href="http://google.com"> <button type = "button">Click Me </button></a>
7       </body>
8    </html>
```

```
 Button                    ×
← → C    file:///l:/button.html

Click Me
```

Form

In HTML, we use form to represent a document section that contains interactive controls to submit information to a web server. The basic structure of HTML form is as shown in the following:

```
<form>
  User ID: <input type = "text"><br>
  Password: <input type ="password"><br>
</form>
```

The output of the code will be as follows:

```
1    <html>
2       <head>
3          <title>Form</title>
4       </head>
5       <body>
6          <form>
7    User ID: <input type = "text"><br>
8    Password: <input type ="password"><br>
9       </form>
10      </body>
11   </html>
12
```

Let's dive little bit deeper now!

If statement

Let's say John has 23 apples and Tom has 45 apples. We want to check who has more apples using JavaScript programming. We need to make our browser understand the **if statement**.

 The if statement compares two variables.

To check our condition, we need to declare the two variables containing the number of apples, as follows:

```
var john = 23;
var tom = 45;
```

To check which number is bigger, we can apply the if statement as shown in the following:

```
if(john > tom)
{
  alert("John has more apples than tom");
}
```

Let's say that we do not know which variable is bigger. Then, we need to check both the variables. Therefore, we need to include the following codes to our program:

```
if(tom > john )
{
  alert("Tom has more apples than John");
}
```

The whole code in an HTML page will be as follows:

```
<html>
  <head>
    <title>
      If statement
    </title>
  </head>
  <body>
    <script type="text/javascript">
      var john = 23;
      var tom = 45;
      if(john > tom){
        alert("John has more apples than Tom");
      }
    if(tom> john ){
      alert("Tom has more apples than John");
    }
    </script>
  </body>
</html>
```

The output will be as follows:

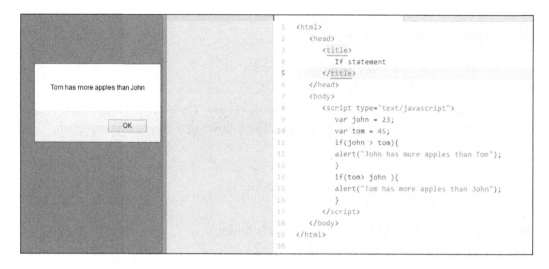

```
1   <html>
2     <head>
3       <title>
4         If statement
5       </title>
6     </head>
7     <body>
8       <script type="text/javascript">
9         var john = 23;
10        var tom = 45;
11        if(john > tom){
12        alert("John has more apples than Tom");
13        }
14        if(tom> john ){
15        alert("Tom has more apples than John");
16        }
17      </script>
18    </body>
19  </html>
20
```

You learned about the conditional operators in the previous chapters. In if statement, you can use all of them. Here are a few examples with comments:

```
If(tom => john){
//This will check if the number of apples are equal or greater.
}
If(tom <= john)
{
//This will check if the number of apples are equal or less.
}
If(tom == john)
{
//This will check if the number of apples are equal.
}
```

To check multiple conditions, you need to use OR (| |) or AND (&&).

Consider the following examples:

```
If(john == 23 || john => tom)
{
/* This will check if John has 23 apples or the number of John's apple
is equal to or greater than Tom's. This condition will be full filled
if any of these two conditions are true.
*/
}
If(tom == 23 && john <= tom)
{
```

```
/* This will check if Tom has 23 apples or the number of john's apple
is less than Tom's or equal. This condition will be full filled if
both of these two conditions are true.
*/
}
```

Switch-case

If you have more than three conditions, it is good practice to use the **switch-case** statement. The basic structure of switch-case is as shown in the following:

```
switch (expression) {
  case expression1:
    break;
  case expression2:
    break;
  case expression3:
    break;
//----------------------------
//----------------------------
//  More case
//----------------------------
//  ----------------------------
  default:
}
```

Every `case` has a `break`. However, the `default` does not need a `break`.

Consider that Tom has 35 pens. His friends John, Cindy, Laura, and Terry have 25, 35, 15, and 18 pens, respectively. Now, John wants to check who has 35 pens. We need to compare the number of Tom's pens with everyone's pens. We can use switch-case for this type of case. The code will be as follows:

```
<html>
  <head>
    <title>
      Switch-Case
    </title>
  </head>
  <body>
    <script type="text/javascript">
      var Tom = 35;
      switch (Tom) {
        case 25: //Number of John's pens
```

```
         document.write("John has equal number of pens as Tom");
         break;
      case 35: //Number of Cindy's pens
         document.write("Cindy has equal number of pens as Tom");
         break;
      case 15: //Number of Laura's pens
         document.write("Laura has equal number of pens as Tom");
         break;
      case 18: //Number of Terry's pens
         document.write("Terry has equal number of pens as Tom");
         break;
      default:
         document.write("No one has equal pens as Tom");
   }
 </script>
 </body>
</html>
```

The output will be as follows:

Cindy has equal number of pens as Tom	

```
1   <html>
2      <head>
3         <title>
4            Switch-Case
5         </title>
6      </head>
7      <body>
8         <script type="text/javascript">
9   var Tom = 35;
10  switch (Tom) {
11    case 25: //Number of John's pens
12       document.write("John has equal number of pens as Tom");
13       break;
14    case 35: //Number of Cindy's pens
15       document.write("Cindy has equal number of pens as Tom");
16       break;
17    case 15: //Number of Laura's pens
18       document.write("Laura has equal number of pens as Tom");
19       break;
20    case 18: //Number of Terry's pens
21       document.write("Terry has equal number of pens as Tom");
22       break;
23    default:
24       document.write("No one has equal pens as Tom");
25  }
26  </script>
27     </body>
28  </html>
```

 Now, change the value of second case (35) to other and check your result.

Exercise

1. Suppose you need to go to school every day except Saturday and Sunday. Write a code, where you will input today's date number and the web page will show you whether you need to go to school or not. (Hint: use a switch case.)

2. Consider that you have a garden and you water all the plants on even days of the month. Write a code that will show you whether you will water your plants on that day. (Hint: use the if condition and modulus operator (%).)

Loops

In this paragraph, we will learn something interesting called **loop**.

Consider that you need to print a line 100 times using JavaScript. What you will do?

You can type `document.write("The line I want You to Write");` 100 times in your program or you can use loop.

The basic use of loop is to do something more than one time. Say, you need to print all the integers of *1 + 2 + 4 + 6 +...........+100* series upto 100. The calculation is the same, you only need to do it multiple times. In these cases, we use loop.

We will discuss two types of loops, namely **for loop** and **while loop**.

The for loop

The basic structure of the for loop is as follows:

```
for(starting ; condition ; increment/decrement)
{
   statement
}
```

The `starting` parameter is the initialization of your loop. You need to initialize the loop in order to start it. The `condition` parameter is the key element to control the loop. The `increment/decrement` parameter defines how your loop will increase/decrease.

Let's see an example. You want to print **javascript is fun** 10 times. The code will be as shown in the following:

```
<html>
  <head>
    <title>For Loop</title>
  </head>
  <body>
  <script type="text/javascript">
    var java;
    for(java=0;java<10;java++){
      document.write("javascript is fun"+"<br>");
    }
  </script>
  </body>
</html>
```

The output will be similar to the following:

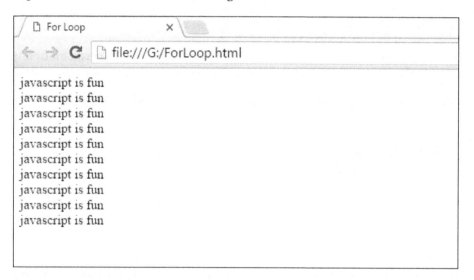

Yes! You printed the line 10 times. If you look at the code carefully, you will see the following:

- We declared a variable named `java`
- In the `for` loop, we initialized `0` to its value
- We added a `java<10` condition that made the browser count from `0` to `10`
- We incremented the variable by 1; that's why we added `java++`

Exercise

1. Write a code using JavaScript that will print the following output:

    ```
    I have 2 apples.
    I have 4 apples.
    I have 6 apples.
    I have 8 apples.
    I have 10 apples.
    I have 12 apples.
    I have 14 apples.
    I have 16 apples.
    I have 18 apples.
    I have 20 apples.
    ```

2. Write a code that will print all the even numbers from 2 to 500.

The while loop

You have already have learned how to execute something multiple times using the for loop. Now, we will learn another loop known as the while loop. The structure of while loop is as follows:

```
initialize;
while(condition){
  statement;
  increment/decrement;
}
```

The codes for the previous example will be like the following:

```
<html>
  <head>
    <title>For Loop</title>
  </head>
  <body>
    <script type="text/javascript">
      var java = 0;
      while(java < 10){
        document.write("javascript is fun"+"<br>");
        java++;
      }
    </script>
  </body>
</html>
```

The output will be the same as the for loop.

Exercise

1. Write a code that will print all the odd values from 1 to 600 using the while loop. (Hint: use the modulus operator.)

2. Write a code that will print the following output:

```
5 x 1  = 5
5 x 2  = 10
5 x 3  = 15
5 x 4  = 20
5 x 5  = 25
5 x 6  = 30
5 x 7  = 35
5 x 8  = 40
5 x 9  = 45
5 x 10 = 50
```

Summary

In this chapter, you learned logical operations using JavaScript. You learned loops, conditional operation, and other HTML tags.

We need to focus on this chapter as we have discussed the most important attributes in JavaScript here. You can become a JavaScript master if you practice this chapter and the last three chapters. I recommend you not to go further unless you have a good knowledge all the four chapters. If you have already learned about all the topics that we discussed earlier, let's move on to *Chapter 5, Ahoy! Sailing into Battle*.

5

Ahoy! Sailing into Battle

In this chapter, we are going to develop a full game using HTML, CSS, and JavaScript. We will focus on the JavaScript coding, therefore, we will not care about the graphics of the game. We will code a game named **Battleship**. Many of you have heard of it before. This is a memory game. Your imagination and intuition will help you to win the game. There are a few variations for playing the game.

Let's discuss how the game looks. There are a few square-shaped geometrical objects connected to each other as shown in the following. The number of rows and columns need to be equal:

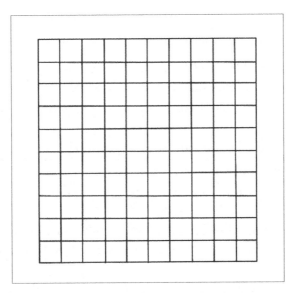

The rows and columns are usually named with the help of number system or alphabets. Let's say that the rows are **1, 2, 3, 4, 5, 6, 7, 8, 9**, and **10**. The columns are **A, B, C, D, E, F, G, H, I**, and **J**. We can name them by either numbers or alphabets:

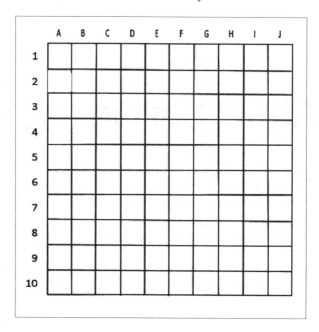

It is a two player game. The following are its rules:

- Both the players will secretly place their ships (there can be different types of boats or water vehicles) on their matrices/grids.

- The players can put their ships vertically or horizontally; however, not diagonally.

- The players must place all their ships on the grid before they start playing.

- Their ships cannot overlap each other's.

- When all the ships are placed, the players cannot move their ships from the grid.

- After placing all the ships, the first player will state a coordinate of the second player and if there is a ship belonging to the second player, the ship will blow.

- Then, the second player will state a coordinate of the first player. If there is a ship belonging to the first player, it will blow.

- The coordinate may look similar to **A2, B2, D5,** and so on. The first alphabet will be the *x* axis of the grids and the number will represent *y* axis of the grid.
- The player that blows all the ships of the opponent will win.

The following figure shows few ships placed on the grid:

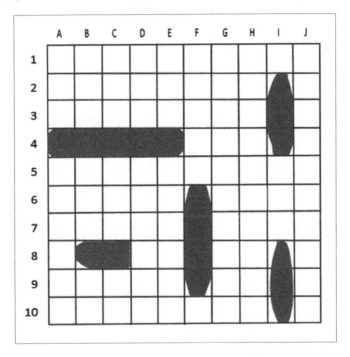

Now, we will head to the programming part of the game.

We will stick to the following rules so that our game does not become difficult to code:

1. There will be one ship belonging to both the players.
2. The ship will occupy four parts of the grid.
3. A player will have to input both the *x* and *y* axes coordinates at the prompt.
4. The grid will be 9 x 9.
5. The player will have to put h or v for the horizontal or vertical position of the ship.

6. To simplify the drawing, we will put dots (.) on the position of the grids. The grids will look similar to the following image:

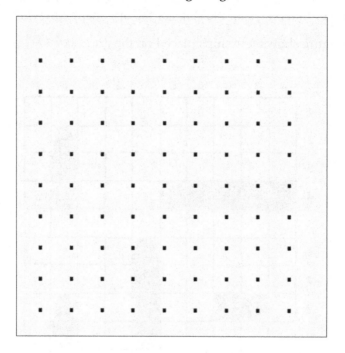

7. We will need a **Fire** button to start the game.

The HTML part

The HTML part will look similar to the following code:

```
<html>
  <head>
  </head>
  <body>
    <h1> Battleship Game </h1>
  </body>
  <style>
// We will code in CSS here
  </style>
  <script type = "text/javascript">
//We will code in JavaScript here
  </script>
</html>
```

The output of the code will be as shown in the following image:

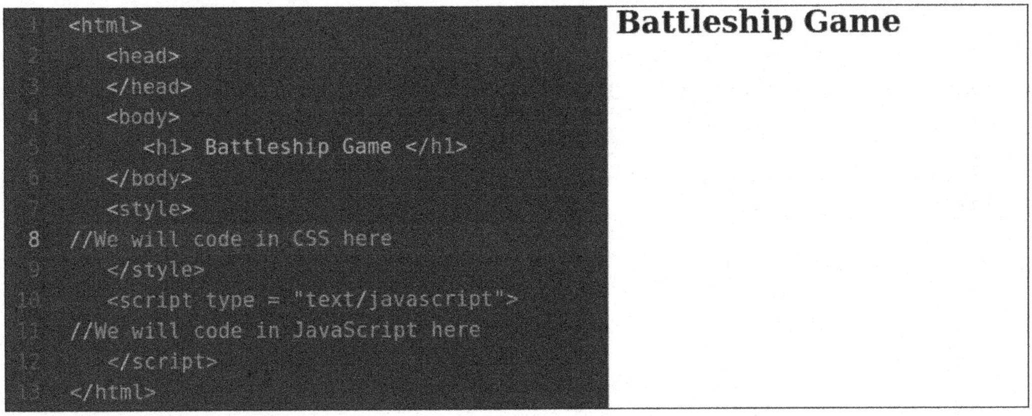

```
1   <html>
2       <head>
3       </head>
4       <body>
5           <h1> Battleship Game </h1>
6       </body>
7       <style>
8   //We will code in CSS here
9       </style>
10      <script type = "text/javascript">
11  //We will code in JavaScript here
12      </script>
13  </html>
```

Battleship Game

The CSS part

We use a CSS coding in the `<style></style>` tags for the body. As we will heed on the coding in JavaScript only, we will not bother about the visual part of the game. To make the body of the game colorful, we will use the following code:

```
<style>
  body {
    background-color: #eff;
  }
</style>
```

The JavaScript part

This part is the main part of our game, we will pay attention to this part the most. We will write all our codes in the `<script></script>` tags.

For the grids, we will need a two dimensional array. We will take a game variable to store the data as follows:

 Many programs may require the processing of multiple data items that have common characteristics. In such situations, it is often convenient to place the data items in an array, where they will all share the same name. The individual data can be characters, floats, integers, and so on. However, they must all be of the same type and class.

```
var game = [    [".", ".", ".", ".", ".", ".", ".", ".", "."],
                [".", ".", ".", ".", ".", ".", ".", ".", "."],
                [".", ".", ".", ".", ".", ".", ".", ".", "."],
                [".", ".", ".", ".", ".", ".", ".", ".", "."],
                [".", ".", ".", ".", ".", ".", ".", ".", "."],
                [".", ".", ".", ".", ".", ".", ".", ".", "."],
                [".", ".", ".", ".", ".", ".", ".", ".", "."],
                [".", ".", ".", ".", ".", ".", ".", ".", "."],
                [".", ".", ".", ".", ".", ".", ".", ".", "."],
            ];
```

We will take a variable to display the two dimensional array on the HTML page:

```
var board = document.createElement("PRE");
```

We will now append this on the body and create a button:

```
document.body.appendChild(board);
var button=document.createElement("BUTTON");
```

This button will call the fire function (we will write the function later.):

```
button.onclick = fire;
```

Now, we will place the button on the body part:

```
var t=document.createTextNode("Fire!");
  document.body.appendChild(button);
  button.appendChild(t);
```

Let's make a function to draw the board:

```
function drawBoard() {
  var boardContents = "";
  var i;
  var j;
  for (i=0; i<9; i++) {
    for (j=0; j<9; j++) {
      boardContents = boardContents + game[i][j]+" ";
      // Append array contents for each board square
    }
    boardContents = boardContents + "<br>";
    // Append a line break at the end of each horizontal line
  }
  return boardContents;
  // Return string representing board in HTML
}
```

Now, put draw the board on the HTML page by writing the following code:

```
board.innerHTML = drawBoard();
```

We will ask the player where he wants to place his ship using the prompt() function:

```
var x=prompt("Where would you like to place your ship? Enter an X
  coordinate: (0-8)");
var y=prompt("Where would you like to place your ship? Enter a Y
  coordinate: (0-8)");
var direction=prompt("Place (h)orizontally, (v)ertically");
x = Number(x);   // Convert the string returned by "prompt" into
  a number
y = Number(y);   // Convert the string returned by "prompt" into
  a number
```

If the player chooses the horizontal orientation for their ship, we need to replace the dots by writing the following code:

```
if (direction[0] == "h") {
  var c;
  for (c = x; c < (x + 4); c++)
  {
    game[y][c] = '#';
  }
}
```

If the player chooses the vertical orientation for their ship, we need to replace the dots by writing the following code:

```
if (direction[0] == "v") {
  var c;
  for (c = y; c < (y + 4); c++)
  {
    game[c][x] = '#';
  }
}
```

We need to redraw the board after placing the ship, as follows:

```
board.innerHTML = drawBoard();
```

Lets create the `fire()` function.

Our `fire()` function will be as follows:

```
function fire() {
//We will write codes here.
}
```

When the `fire()` function is called, we need to take input from the player as shown in the following:

```
var fireX=prompt("Where would you like to fire? Enter an X
  coordinate: (0-8)");
var fireY=prompt("Where would you like to fire? Enter a Y
  coordinate: (0-8)");
```

Convert the inputs into numbers, as follows:

```
fireX = Number(fireX);
// Convert the string returned by "prompt" into a number
fireY = Number(fireY);
//  Convert the string returned by "prompt" into a number
```

If the input does not match with the # character, we will print You Missed. using the following code:

```
if (game[fireY][fireX] == ".") {
  // Check if the specified coordinate is occupied by the
    cruiser
  alert("You Missed.");
}
```

If the input hits the ship, we will print few messages and draw the board again:

```
else if (game[fireY][fireX] == "*") {
  alert("You already hit the ship there.");
} else {
  alert("Kaboom! You hit a ship");
  game[fireY][fireX] = "*";
  board.innerHTML = drawBoard();
  // Redraw board with hit marker at specified coordinate
}
```

Now, we need to check whether there is any ship remaining on the board. We will use the following code:

```
var shipfound;
var i;
var j;
// Check if there are any ships remaining on the board
for (i=0; i<9; i++) {
  for (j=0; j<9; j++) {
    if (game[i][j] != "." && game[i][j] != "*") {
      shipfound = true;
      // Taking a boolean data type to set it if a ship is found
    }
  }
}
```

If no ship is left, we will end the game:

```
if (!shipfound) {
  // If no ships are found end the game
  alert("All ships have been sunk. Well done Captain! Game over");
  document.body.removeChild(button);
  // Remove the fire button from the page after game over
}
```

The final code

Our final codes will look similar to the following:

```
<html>
  <head>
  </head>
  <body>
    <h1> Battleship Game </h1>
```

```
    </body>
    <style>
    body {
      background-color: #eff;
    }
    </style>
    <script>
      var game = [   [".", ".", ".", ".", ".", ".", ".", ".", "."],
                     [".", ".", ".", ".", ".", ".", ".", ".", "."],
                     [".", ".", ".", ".", ".", ".", ".", ".", "."],
                     [".", ".", ".", ".", ".", ".", ".", ".", "."],
                     [".", ".", ".", ".", ".", ".", ".", ".", "."],
                     [".", ".", ".", ".", ".", ".", ".", ".", "."],
                     [".", ".", ".", ".", ".", ".", ".", ".", "."],
                     [".", ".", ".", ".", ".", ".", ".", ".", "."],
                     [".", ".", ".", ".", ".", ".", ".", ".", "."],
                 ];
      var board = document.createElement("PRE");
      // preparing the HTML <pre> element to display the board on
        the page
      document.body.appendChild(board);
      var button=document.createElement("BUTTON");
      // Preparing the "Fire! button to allow the player to fire at
        the ship
      button.onclick = fire;        // Clicking the button calls the
fire() function
      var t=document.createTextNode("Fire!");
      document.body.appendChild(button);
      button.appendChild(t);
      function drawBoard() {
        var boardContents = "";
        var i;  var j;
        for (i=0; i<9; i++) {
          for (j=0; j<9; j++) {
            boardContents = boardContents + game[i][j]+" ";
            // Append array contents for each board square
          }
          boardContents = boardContents + "<br>";
          // Append a line break at the end of each horizontal line
        }  return boardContents;
        // Return string representing board in HTML
      }
      board.innerHTML = drawBoard();
      // Display the board on the page using the above function
```

```
var x=prompt("Where would you like to place your cruiser?
  Enter an X coordinate: (0-8)");
var y=prompt("Where would you like to place your cruiser?
  Enter a Y coordinate: (0-8)");
var direction=prompt("Place (h)orizontally, (v)ertically");
x = Number(x);  // Convert the string returned by "prompt"
  into a number
y = Number(y);  // Convert the string returned by "prompt"
  into a number
if (direction[0] == "h") {
  var c;
  for (c = x; c < (x + 4); c++)
  {
    game[y][c] = '4';
  }
}
// Draw cruiser vertically
if (direction[0] == "v") {
  var c;
  for (c = y; c < (y + 4); c++)
  {
    game[c][x] = '4';
  }
}
board.innerHTML = drawBoard(); // Redraw board with cruiser
  added
// Function for firing a shot when the "Fire! button is
  pressed
function fire() {
  var fireX=prompt("Where would you like to fire? Enter an X
    coordinate: (0-8)");
  var fireY=prompt("Where would you like to fire? Enter a Y
    coordinate: (0-8)");
  fireX = Number(fireX);
  // Convert the string returned by "prompt" into a number
  fireY = Number(fireY);
  //  Convert the string returned by "prompt" into a number
  if (game[fireY][fireX] == ".") {
    // Check if the specified coordinate is occupied by the
      cruiser
    alert("Missed.");
  }
  else if (game[fireY][fireX] == "*") {
    alert("You already hit the ship there.");
  } else {
```

```
            alert("Kaboom! You hit a ship");
            game[fireY][fireX] = "*";
            board.innerHTML = drawBoard();
            // Redraw board with hit marker at specified coordinate
          }
        var shipfound;
        var i;
        var j;
        // Check if there are any ships remaining on the board
        for (i=0; i<9; i++) {
          for (j=0; j<9; j++) {
            if (game[i][j] != "." && game[i][j] != "*") {
              shipfound = true;
              // Set to true if a ship is found
            }
          }
        }if (!shipfound) {
          // If no ships are found end the game
          alert("All ships have been sunk. Well done Captain! Game
            over");
          document.body.removeChild(button);
          // Remove the fire button from the page after game over
        }
      }
    </script>
  </html>
```

If you run the preceding code, you will see the following prompt:

Let's play the game that we created. The first player has to place his ship. He has to input the coordinates of the ship.

Consider that we input 3 on the *x* axis and 2 on the *y* axis. Place our ship on the vertical orientation. The game screen will look as shown in the following:

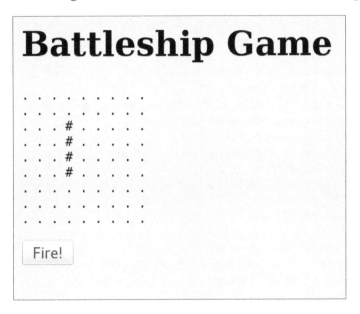

You can see that your ship is placed. Now, you can shoot your opponent (computer) by pressing the **Fire** button. You will be asked to input the coordinates of the grid, where you want to shoot. If you miss a shot, you will see a message that we coded, **You Missed.**

I hope that you are able to play the game that you built.

Congratulations!

If you want to develop your game more (such as enhance the graphics, number of ships, and so on), you only need to develop CSS and JavaScript.

Now, we will see a better code for the Battleship game, as shown in the following:

1. Make a js folder anywhere in your computer.

2. In the js folder, place the three files that are included in this chapter: battleship.js, functions.js, and jquery.min.js.

3. Outside the js folder, place the battleship.css and index.html files.

Open the `index.html` file in a Notepad, you will see the following code:

```
<html>
  <head>
    <title>Battleship</title>
    <meta name="viewport" content="width=device-width" />
    <link href="battleship.css" rel="stylesheet" type="text/css"/>
  </head>
  <body>
    <h1>BATTLESHIP</h1>
    <div class="game-types">
      <h2 class='game-choice'>Choose a game type</h2>
      <dl class="game-description">
        <dt>Standard</dt>
        <dd>Classic Battleship with randomly placed ships</dd>
        <dt>Custom</dt>
        <dd>Choose any 5 ships and place them where you like.
          The computer will have the same 5 ships, randomly
          placed</dd>
      </dl>
      <div class='button-wrapper'>
        <button class="standard">Standard</button>
        <button class="custom">Custom</button>
      </div>
    </div>
    <div class='ship-picker'>
      <h2>Pick 5 Ships</h2>
      <h3>Selected ships</h3>
      <ul class="ship-list">
        <li>
          <p></p>
          <div class='remove'>X</div>
        </li>
        <li>
          <p></p>
          <div class='remove'>X</div>
        </li>
        <li>
          <p></p>
          <div class='remove'>X</div>
        </li>
        <li>
          <p></p>
          <div class='remove'>X</div>
        </li>
```

```
      <li>
        <p></p>
        <div class='remove'>X</div>
      </li>
    </ul>
    <ul class='ship-choices button-wrapper'>
      <li class="ship-choice">Carrier</li>
      <li class="ship-choice">Battleship</li>
      <li class="ship-choice">Submarine</li>
      <li class="ship-choice">Cruiser</li>
      <li class="ship-choice">Destroyer</li>
    </ul>
    <div class='button-wrapper'>
      <button class='build-fleet inactive'>Build Fleet</button>
    </div>
  </div>
  <div class="ship-placer">
    <div class="board placer-board">
      <div class="labels">
        <div class="row-label">
        </div>
        <div class="column-label">
        </div>
      </div>
      <div class="playable-area">
      </div>
    </div>
    <div class='ships-to-place'>
      <h3>Ships to place</h3>
      <ul>
      </ul>
    </div>

    <div class="clear"></div>
    <div class="instructions">
      <p>Use 'WASD' keys to rotate pieces</p>
    </div>

    <div class='button-wrapper'>
      <button class="start inactive">Start game</button>
    </div>
  </div>
  <div class="game-area">
    <div class="board-wrap">
```

```
        <h1 class="hidden">BATTLESHIP</h1>
        <div class="single-board-wrap">
          <div class="board human-board">
            <div class="labels">
              <div class="row-label">
              </div>
              <div class="column-label">
              </div>
            </div>
            <div class="playable-area">
            </div>
          </div>
          <h2>Human Board</h2>
        </div>
        <div class="single-board-wrap">
          <div class="board ai-board">
            <div class="labels">
              <div class="row-label">
              </div>
              <div class="column-label">
              </div>
            </div>
            <div class="playable-area">
            </div>
          </div>
          <h2>Opponent Board</h2>
        </div>
        <div class="button-wrapper">
          <button class="new-game">New Game</button>
          <button class="stats hidden">Show Stats</button>
        </div>
      </div>
      <div class="info-area">
        <h2>Enemy ships remaining</h2>
        <div class="scoreboard">
          <div class="ships-left">
          </div>
        </div>
        <div class="gamelog-container">
          <h2>GAME LOG</h2>
        </div>
      </div>
    </div>
    <script src="js/jquery.min.js"></script>
```

```
        <script src="js/functions.js"></script>
        <script src="js/battleship.js"></script>
    </body>
</html>
```

We included the three JavaScript files in the HTML file. We added a jQuery file, which we will discuss in the next chapter. The output of the preceding code will show you the following screen:

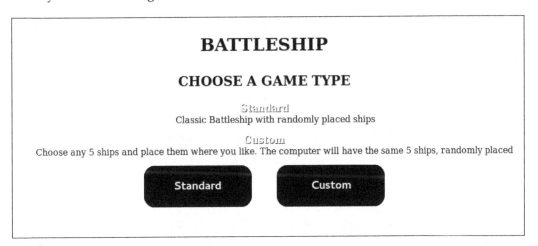

You can click the **Standard** button to play the standard Battlefield or **Custom** button to play a non-standard Battlefield.

If you select the **Standard** button, you will get the following screen:

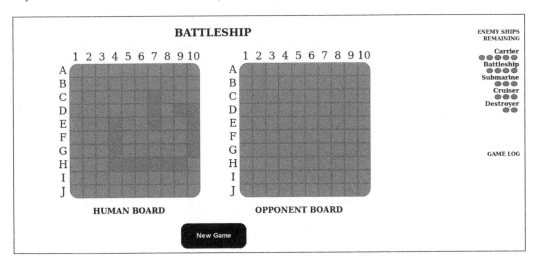

Now, you can guess the position of the opponent's ship and click on the grid. There will be a log panel on the right-hand side of the screen. You can also see how many and which ships you have destroyed from the preceding panel of the game log panel.

If you select the **Custom** play, you will see the following screen:

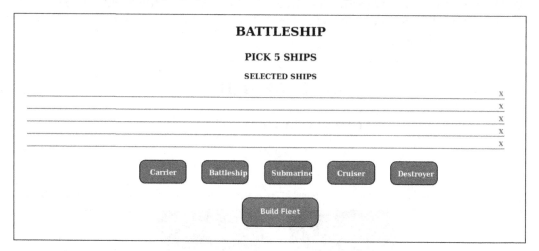

After adding the five ships, you can play the game. You can add the same ship twice or more, if required.

You can place your ships vertically or horizontally and click on the tiles to blow the opponent's ship. You can click one tile at a time.

Summary

In this chapter, we built a complete game and played it. We also played a better version of the game we have built. All you need to remember is that you must know the logic behind all the code that we previously discussed. You are given the source code of the better version of the game with this chapter. I hope that you will study the code and write your own Battleship game. We used a `jquery.js` JavaScript file on our improved version of the Battleship. The `jquery.js` file has a lot of lines of code (We will discuss this in *Chapter 6, Exploring the Benefits of jQuery*).

If you master all the code that we discussed in this chapter, we can now move to the next chapter.

6
Exploring the Benefits of jQuery

If you have gone through the previous chapter, you probably have implemented **jQuery** in your **Battleship** game. In this chapter, we will discuss about jQuery in detail.

The jQuery library is a JavaScript framework. It was released in 2006. People used to call it **jSelect**. We use jQuery in our websites so that we can work with JavaScript easily and add effects to our web pages. You may think jQuery is different from JavaScript. No! jQuery is just another JavaScript file. It is a very lightweight library that helps you to decorate your web pages more easily with less coding.

We use jQuery due to the following advantages:

- It is open source; you can edit or modify its code if required
- It is a small library (about 150 KB file)
- The community support for jQuery is very strong; you can get help from the users easily
- It is user-friendly and popular
- It supports cross-browsers
- It is openly developed; you can fix any bug or add features to it by editing the codes
- It helps the developers to build responsive sites by using AJAX
- It has built-in animation functions that help a developer to create animations in their website

Installing jQuery

The question is where to find jQuery. Well, you can find it at http://jquery.com/. I have also attached the file with this book. You can download it from there.

If you go to http://jquery.com/, you will see the following screen:

Click the **Download jQuery** button. You will be redirected to the following page:

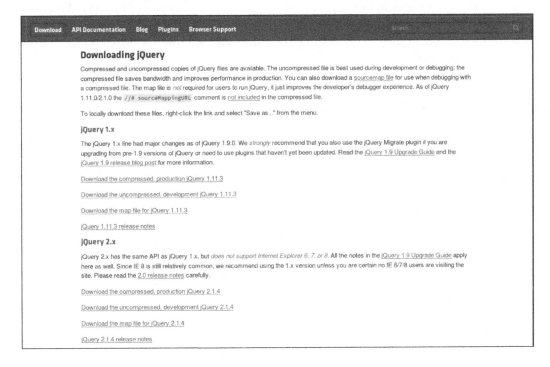

There are two versions of jQuery: `1.x.x` and `2.x.x`. There are just a few differences between these versions. The compressed version's code is not readable as the version does not have blank spaces and comments; however, the uncompressed version is clearly coded and formatted, it also has important comments to understand the code and functions' work. If you want to learn how a function of jQuery works, I would suggest you to go through the jQuery uncompressed version.

Throughout this chapter, we will use the `2.x.x` version. The latest version of `2.x.x` is `2.2.0`.

 You can download the compressed or uncompressed version of jQuery. I'll advice you to use the compressed version as it is lightweight.

We will use the uncompressed version for this chapter so that you can study the `jquery.js` and get a clear concept of how it works. After clicking **Download the uncompressed, development jQuery** 2.2.0, you will see the jQuery library on your browser. Click *Ctrl + S* on your keyboard to save the file, as shown in the following screenshot:

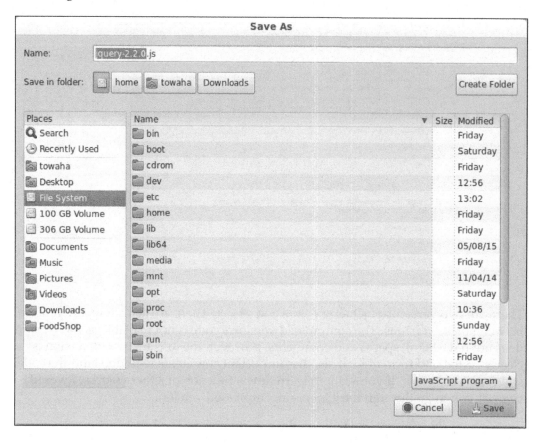

After downloading the jQuery, place it in your computer. For simplicity, rename it to `jquery`.

Create a new HTML file in the same folder and include the `jquery.js` in your HTML document by typing the following code in the `<head></head>` tags:

```
<script src="jquery.js"></script>
```

To check whether your imported `jquery.js` is working, type the following code. I will explain the code later:

```html
<html>
  <head>
    <script type="text/JavaScript" src="jquery.js"></script>
  </head>
  <script type="text/JavaScript">
    jQuery(document).ready(function()
    {
      jQuery('h1').click(function()
      {
        alert("jQuery is working!");
      } //click function ends here.
      );
    } // ready function ends here.
    );
  </script>
  <body>
    <h1>Click Here!</h1>
  </body>
</html>
```

After opening the HTML file, click on **Click Here!** You will see the following screen:

It means your jQuery is working.

Let's discuss the code that we have written.

 You can also install jQuery without downloading it. This kind of installation is known as **content delivery network (CDN)** installation.

You need to add the following line to your HTML document and if you're connected online, your browser will automatically load jQuery.

```
<script type = "text/javascript" src =
    "http://ajax.googleapis.com/ajax/libs/
    jquery/2.1.3/jquery.min.js"></script>
```

Explaining the code

Now, let's discuss the code that we previously used. We used the following function in our code:

```
jQuery(document).ready(function(){
//our codes.
});
```

This is a jQuery function that allows you to set your jQuery ready to be used. You can replace jQuery with a dollar sign ($) as shown in the following:

```
$(document).ready(function(){
//our codes.
});
```

You need to think where you want to apply jQuery. We have written <h1>Click Here!</h1> in our body tags. We wanted our Click Here! to do something when clicked and that's why we added a click function similar to the following format:

```
jQuery('h1').click(function(){
    //our codes.
});
```

The jQuery can be replaced with $ as earlier mentioned.

We added an alert function so that when we click on our text, there appears an alert box.

Going deeper

Let's discuss jQuery functions/methods that we use frequently in detail.

All the methods should be written in the `ready()` function. Some of the commonly used methods are as follows:

- Load
- Keyup
- Keydown
- Change
- Focus
- Blur
- Resize
- Scroll

The load() method

Using this method, you can load a file on your browser. Consider that you want to fetch some text from a `.txt` file on your browser. You can do the following coding:

```html
<html>
  <head>
    <script type="text/JavaScript" src="jquery.js"></script>
  </head>
  <script>
    $(document).ready(function(){
      $("button").click(function(){
        $("#click").load("test.txt");
      });
    });
  </script>
  <body>
    <div id="click">
      Hello;
    </div>
    <button type="button" name="button">Click to replace "Hello" from
      text file</button>
  </body>
</html>
```

After clicking the button, the text in the `click` div will be changed to
Congratulations! You have loaded your file!!, as shown in the following:

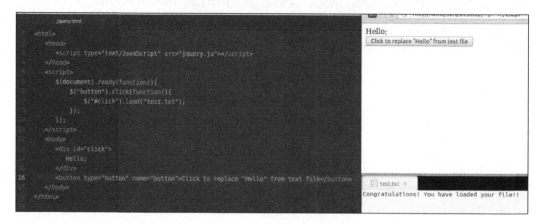

The keyup() and keydown() methods

Using this method, you can control your keyboard buttons' key-pressing. You can
make your browser do something when a key is pressed or not pressed. Consider
that you have a textbox and you want to take an input from there. When the keys are
pressed, you want your textbox to change to red color; otherwise the color should
remain green. You can do this by implementing/writing the following code:

```html
<html>
  <head>
    <script type="text/JavaScript" src="jquery.js"></script>
  </head>
  <script>
    $(document).ready(function(){
      $("input").keydown(function(){
        $("input").css("background-color", "green");
      });
      $("input").keyup(function(){
        $("input").css("background-color", "red");
      });
    });
  </script>
  <body>
    Type Something:   <input type="text">
  </body>
</html>
```

The change() method

To change some text, you can use this method by implementing the following code:

```html
<html>
  <head>
    <script type="text/JavaScript" src="jquery.js"></script>
  </head>
  <script>
$(document).ready(function(){
  $("input").change(function(){
    alert("The text has been changed.");
  });
});
  </script>
  <body>
    Type Something:   <input type="text">
  </body>
</html>
```

Your output will look similar to the following image:

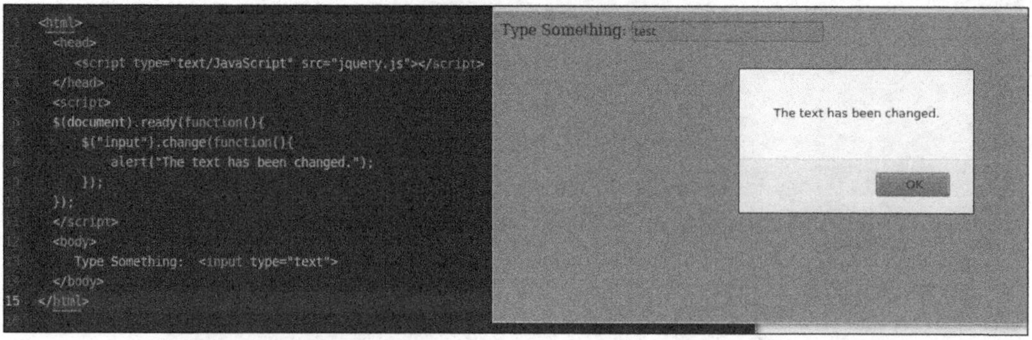

The blur() and focus() methods

To make your text or button blurred or focused, you can implement the following code:

```html
<html>
  <head>
    <script type="text/JavaScript" src="jquery.js"></script>
  </head>
  <script>
$(document).ready(function(){
  $("button").blur(function(){
    alert("Your button is not focused!");
  });
});
  </script>
  <body>
    <button type="button">CLick Me!</button>
  </body>
</html>
```

You can do this for the `focus()` method too, as follows:

```
<html>
<head>
    <script type="text/JavaScript" src="jquery.js"></script>
</head>
<script>
$(document).ready(function(){
    $("button").blur(function(){
        alert("Your button is not focused!");
    });
});
</script>
<body>
    <button type="button">Click Me!</button>
</body>
</html>
```

Click Me!

Your button is not focused!

OK

The resize() method

If you want to see how many times your browser is resized, you can do the following on your HTML document:

```
1  <html>
2  <head>
3  <script src="jquery.js"></script>
4  <script>
5  x = 0;
6  $(document).ready(function(){
7      $(window).resize(function(){
8          $("p").text("You resized your window");
9      });
10 });
11 </script>
12 </head>
13 <body>
14 <p>Ctrl+Scroll or press ctrl + ++ to resize the window</p>
15 </body>
16 </html>
17
```

You resized your window

The scroll() method

You can add actions to the mouse scrolling using the following code:

```
<html>
  <head>
    <script src="jquery.js"></script>
    <script>
      $(document).ready(function(){
        $("div").scroll(function(){
          $("span").text("You are scrolling!");
        });
```

```
        });
      </script>
    </head>
    <body>
      <div style="border:2px solid black;width:200px;
        height:200px;overflow:scroll;">
        Cowards die many times before their deaths;<br>
        The valiant never taste of death but once.<br>
        Of all the wonders that I yet have heard,<br>
        It seems to me most strange that men should fear;<br>
        Seeing that death, a necessary end,<br>
        Will come when it will come.<br>
      </div>
      <span></span>
    </body>
</html>
```

When you scroll with your mouse, you can see the event that you created in the `scroll()` function, as follows:

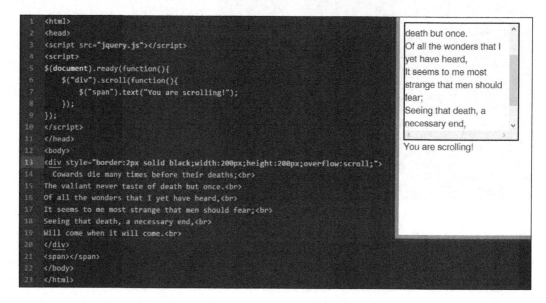

Summary

The jQuery library is super fun to use and easy for new learners. All you have to do is practice the methods and functions of jQuery. There are a lot of jQuery plugins online. You can also download and install them to your web page. Using jQuery and its plugins, you can beautifully decorate and code your site easily. The most interesting part of jQuery, for me, is animation. I will explain how to animate things using jQuery in the next chapter.

7
Introducing the Canvas

In this chapter, we are going to learn about HTML canvas. An HTML canvas helps you to draw, especially the graphics (for example, circles, squares, rectangles, and so on) on your HTML page. The `<canvas></canvas>` tags are usually controlled by JavaScript. Canvas can draw texts, which can also be animated. Let's see what we can do using the HTML canvas.

Implementing canvas

To add canvas on your HTML page, you need to define the height and width of your canvas in the `<canvas></canvas>` tags as shown in the following:

```
<html>
  <head>
    <title>Canvas</title>
  </head>
  <body>
  <canvas id="canvasTest" width="200" height="100"
    style="border:2px solid #000;">

    </canvas>
  </body>
</html>
```

We have defined the canvas ID as `canvasTest`, which will be used to play with the canvas. We used inline CSS on our canvas. The 2 px solid border is used to have a better view of the canvas.

Adding JavaScript

Now, we are going to add few lines of JavaScript for our canvas. We need to add our JavaScript just after the `<canvas></canvas>` tags in the `<script></script>` tags.

Drawing a rectangle

To test our canvas, let's draw a rectangle in the canvas by typing the following code:

```
<script type="text/javascript">
  var canvas = document.getElementById("canvasTest"); //called our
    canvas by id
  var canvasElement = canvas.getContext("2d"); // made our canvas
    2D
  canvasElement.fillStyle = "black"; //Filled the canvas black
  canvasElement.fillRect(10, 10, 50, 50); //created a rectangle
</script>
```

In the script, we declared two JavaScript variables. The `canvas` variable is used to hold the content of our canvas using the canvas ID, which we used in our `<canvas></canvas>` tags. The `canvasElement` variable is used to hold the context of the canvas. We assign `black` to `fillstyle` so that the rectangle that we want to draw turns black when filled. We used `canvasElement.fillRect(x, y, w, h);` for the shape of the rectangle. Where x is the distance of the rectangle from the x axis; y is the distance of the rectangle from the y axis; and `w` and `h` are the width and height of the rectangle, respectively.

The full code is as shown in the following:

```
<html>
  <head>
    <title>Canvas</title>
  </head>
  <body>
    <canvas id="canvasTest" width="200" height="100"
      style="border:2px solid #000;">
    </canvas>
    <script type="text/javascript">
      var canvas = document.getElementById("canvasTest"); //called
        our canvas by id
      var canvasElement = canvas.getContext("2d"); // made our
        canvas 2D
      canvasElement.fillStyle = "black"; //Filled the canvas black
      canvasElement.fillRect(10, 10, 50, 50); //created a
        rectangle
```

```
        </script>
      </body>
    </html>
```

The output of the code is as follows:

Drawing a line

To draw a line in the canvas that you need to insert the following code in your `<script></script>` tags:

```
<script type="text/javascript">
   var c = document.getElementById("canvasTest");
   var canvasElement = c.getContext("2d");
   canvasElement.moveTo(0,0);
   canvasElement.lineTo(100,100);
   canvasElement.stroke();
</script>
```

Here, `canvasElement.moveTo(0,0);` is used to have our line start from the (0,0) co-ordinate of our canvas. The `canvasElement.lineTo(100,100);` statement is used to make the line diagonal. The `canvasElement.stroke();` statement is used to make the line visible. I would suggest you to change the numbers in `canvasElement.lineTo(100,100);` and `canvasElement.moveTo(0,0);` and see the changes to your line drawn by canvas.

The following is the output of the code:

A quick exercise

1. Draw a line using canvas and JavaScript, which will be parallel to the *y* axis of the canvas.

2. Draw a rectangle having 300 px height and 200 px width. Draw a line on the same canvas, touching the rectangle.

Drawing a circle

To draw a circle in the canvas, you need to add the following code in your `<script></script>` tags:

```
<script type="text/javascript">
  var c = document.getElementById("canvasTest");
  var canvasElement = c.getContext("2d");
  canvasElement.beginPath();
  canvasElement.arc(95,50,40,0,2*Math.PI);
  canvasElement.stroke();
</script>
```

Here, we used `canvasElement.beginPath();` to start drawing the circle, `canvasElement.arc(95,50,40,0,2*Math.PI);` for the shape of the circle, and `canvasElement.stroke();` to set the circle visible.

The canvasElement.arc(95,50,40,0,2*Math.PI); statement is similar to canvasElement.arc(x, y, r, sA, eA, ac);,

where x is the starting coordinate from *x* axis, y is the starting coordinate from *y* axis, r is the radius of the circle, sA is the starting angle of the circle, eA is the ending angle of the circle, and ac is the direction of the circle. Here, ac denotes anticlockwise.

The output of our code will be the following image:

Draw linear gradient

Let's draw something new. We will draw a rectangle and make its color fade gradually. Type the following code in your <script></script> tags:

```
<script type="text/javascript">
  var c = document.getElementById("canvasTest");
  var canvasElement = c.getContext("2d");
  // Create the gradient
  var grdient = canvasElement.createLinearGradient(0,0,100,0);
  grdient.addColorStop(0,"blue"); // here we added blue as our
    primary color
  grdient.addColorStop(1,"white"); //here we used white as our
    secondary color.
  // Fill with gradient
  canvasElement.fillStyle = grdient;
  canvasElement.fillRect(10,10,150,80);
</script>
```

We added canvasElement.createLinearGradient(0,0,100,0); to create the gradient or fading. We added grdient.addColorStop(0,"blue"); and grdient.addColorStop(1,"white"); to color the rectangle.

The output of the code is as shown in the following image:

A quick exercise

1. Draw the following smiley face using HTML canvas. (**Hint**: you will have to draw three full circles and a half circle. The trick is that you can draw the figure by playing with the code of circle for the canvas.):

2. Draw a circle with a color gradient.

Let's make a clock!

We are going to draw an analog clock and make it work as a real clock. In your body part of the HTML document, type the following code:

```
<canvas id="myclock" height="500" width="500"></canvas>
In your <script></script> tags, take the following variables:
Var canvas; // the clock canvas
```

```
var canvasElement; // canvas's elements

// clock settings
var cX = 0;
var cY = 0;
var radius = 150;
```

Here, `cX` and `cY` are the center coordinates of our clock. We took 150 px as the clock's radius. You can increase or decrease it.

Then, we need to initialize the variables. Make an `init()`; function after defining the preceding variables.

The function should look similar to the following:

```
function init() {

    canvas = document.getElementById("myclock");
    //Called the element to work on.
    canvasElement = canvas.getContext("2d");
    //Made the context 2d.

    cX = canvas.width / 2;
    // we divided by two to get the middle point of X-axis
    cY = canvas.height / 2;
    // we divided by two to get the middle point of Y-axis
    initTime(); //called the initTime() function.
    drawClock(); //Called the drawClock() function to draw the
      graphics.

    setInterval("animateClock()", 1000); // Made the animation for
      each second. Here 1000 is equal to 1 second.

}
```

Let's initialize the second, minute, and hour hands of our clock:

```
function initTime() {
  date = new Date();
  hours = date.getHours() % 12; // Divided by 12 to make our clock
    12 hours.
  minutes = date.getMinutes();
  seconds = date.getSeconds();

}
```

Here, `date.getHours()`, `date.getMinutes()`, and `date.getSeconds()` will return your computer's time and save them on our variables.

Make another function that will animate our clock:

```
function animateClock() {
  //This function will help our 'second' hand to move after an
    interval.
  clearCanvas(); // This will clear the canvas
  refreshTime(); // This will refresh time after 1 second.
  drawClock();   // This will draw the clock.

}
```

We will write `clearCanvas()`, `refreshTime()`, and `drawClock()` now:

```
function clearCanvas() {
  canvasElement.clearRect(0, 0, canvas.width, canvas.height);
}
```

Here, `canvasElement.clearRect(0, 0, canvas.width, canvas.height);` will reset our canvas after a definite time interval.

Our `refreshTime()` function should look as shown in the following:

```
function refreshTime() {
  seconds += 1;
  if (Math.floor((seconds / 60)) != 0) { //we divide seconds by 60
    until second is equal to zero.
    minutes += 1; // If 60 second is passed we increment minute by
      1.
    seconds %= 60;
  }
  if (Math.floor((minutes / 60)) != 0) {
    hours += 1; //We increment hour by 1 after 60 minutes.
    minutes %= 60;
  }
}
```

We incremented our `seconds` variable in the `refreshTime()` function. Therefore, whenever this function is called, our variable will be incremented by 1. Then, we have done two conditional operations for our `hours` and `minutes`.

Now, let's draw the clock:

```
function drawClock() {
  drawClockBackground(); //This draws clock background.
```

```
    drawSecondsHand(); //This draws clock's second hand.
    drawMinutesHand(); //This draws clock's minute hand.
    drawHoursHand(); //This draws clock's hour hand.
}
```

We will write the `drawClockBackground()`, `drawSecondsHand()`, `drawMinutesHand()`, and `drawHoursHand()` functions:

```
function drawClockBackground() {
    //this function will draw the background of our clock. We are
      declaring few variables for mathematical purposes.
    var correction = 1/300;
    var shift_unit = 1/170;
    var shift_factor = 1/30;
    var angle_initial_position = 2;
    var angle_current_position_begin = 0;
    var angle_current_position_end = 0;
    var repeat = 60;
    var lineWidth = 10;

    for (var i=0; i < repeat; i+=1) {
    //These lines are written for making our clock error free with
      the angle of the hands (hands' positions)
    angle_current_position_begin = angle_initial_position - (i *
      shift_factor) - correction;
    angle_current_position_end = angle_current_position_begin +
      shift_unit;

    if (i % 5 === 0)
    lineWidth = 20;
    else
    lineWidth = 10;

    drawArcAtPosition(cX, cY, radius,
      angle_current_position_begin*Math.PI,
      angle_current_position_end*Math.PI, false, lineWidth);
    }
    drawLittleCircle(cX, cY);
}
```

We performed some mathematical things in this function and wrote the `drawLittleCircle(cX, cY)` function for a little circle on the center of our clock.

The function should look similar to the following:

```
function drawLittleCircle(cX, cY) {
    drawArcAtPosition(cX, cY, 4, 0*Math.PI, 2*Math.PI, false, 4);
}
```

Write the `drawSecondsHand()` function. This function will draw the second hand, as follows:

```
function drawSecondsHand() {
    /* Simple mathematics to find the co ordinate of the second
       hand;
       You may know this: x = rcos(theta), y = rsin(theta). We used
          these here.
       We divided the values n=by 30 because after 5 seconds the
          second hand moves 30 degree.
    */
    endX = cX + radius*Math.sin(seconds*Math.PI / 30);
    endY = cY - radius*Math.cos(seconds*Math.PI / 30);
    drawHand(cX, cY, endX, endY);
}
```

Our `drawMinutesHand()` function should look as shown in the following. This function will draw the minute hand of our clock, as follows:

```
function drawMinutesHand() {
    var rotationUnit = minutes + seconds / 60;
    var rotationFactor = Math.PI / 30;
    var rotation = rotationUnit*rotationFactor;
    var handLength = 0.8*radius;
    endX = cX + handLength*Math.sin(rotation);
    endY = cY - handLength*Math.cos(rotation);
    drawHand(cX, cY, endX, endY);
}
```

Now, let's see our `drawHoursHand();` function. This function will draw the hour hand:

```
function drawHoursHand() {
    var rotationUnit = 5 * hours + minutes / 12;
    var rotationFactor = Math.PI / 30;
    var rotation = rotationUnit*rotationFactor;
    var handLength = 0.4*radius;

    endX = cX + handLength*Math.sin(rotation);
    endY = cY - handLength*Math.cos(rotation);
    drawHand(cX, cY, endX, endY);
}
```

We used a `drawHand();` function in the preceding functions. Let's write the function, as follows:

```
function drawHand(beginX, beginY, endX, endY) {
  canvasElement.beginPath();
  canvasElement.moveTo(beginX, beginY);
  canvasElement.lineTo(endX, endY);
  canvasElement.stroke();
  canvasElement.closePath();
}
```

Now, we are going to write the last function for our clock, as shown in the following snippet:

```
function drawArcAtPosition(cX, cY, radius, start_angle, end_angle,
  counterclockwise, lineWidth) {
  canvasElement.beginPath();
  canvasElement.arc(cX, cY, radius, start_angle, end_angle,
    counterclockwise);
  canvasElement.lineWidth = lineWidth;
  canvasElement.strokeStyle = "black";
  canvasElement.stroke();
  canvasElement.closePath();
}
```

The full code of our clock should look similar to the following code:

```
<html>
  <head>
    <script type="text/javascript">
      var canvas;
      var canvasElement;

      // clock settings
      var cX = 0;

      var cY = 0;
      var radius = 150;

      // time settings
      var date;
      var hours;
      var minutes;
      var seconds;

      function init() {
```

```
canvas = document.getElementById("myclock");
canvasElement = canvas.getContext("2d");

cX = canvas.width / 2;
cY = canvas.height / 2;

initTime();
drawClock();
setInterval("animateClock()", 1000);
}

// get your system time
function initTime() {
  date = new Date();
  hours = date.getHours() % 12;
  minutes = date.getMinutes();
  seconds = date.getSeconds();
}

// animate the clock
function animateClock() {
  clearCanvas();
  refreshTime();
  drawClock();
}

// clear the canvas
function clearCanvas() {
  canvasElement.clearRect(0, 0, canvas.width,
    canvas.height);
}

// refresh time after 1 second
function refreshTime() {
  seconds += 1;
  if (Math.floor((seconds / 60)) != 0) { minutes += 1;
    seconds %= 60; }
  if (Math.floor((minutes / 60)) != 0) { hours += 1; minutes
    %= 60; }
}

// draw or redraw Clock after time refresh function is
  called
function drawClock() {
  drawClockBackground();
```

```
    drawSecondsHand();
    drawMinutesHand();
    drawHoursHand();
}
function drawHand(beginX, beginY, endX, endY) {
  canvasElement.beginPath();
  canvasElement.moveTo(beginX, beginY);
  canvasElement.lineTo(endX, endY);
  canvasElement.stroke();
  canvasElement.closePath();
}

// draw Hand for seconds
function drawSecondsHand() {
  endX = cX + radius*Math.sin(seconds*Math.PI / 30);
  endY = cY - radius*Math.cos(seconds*Math.PI / 30);
  drawHand(cX, cY, endX, endY);
}

// draw Hand for minutes
function drawMinutesHand() {
  var rotationUnit = minutes + seconds / 60;
  var rotationFactor = Math.PI / 30;
  var rotation = rotationUnit*rotationFactor;
  var handLength = 0.8*radius;

  endX = cX + handLength*Math.sin(rotation);
  endY = cY - handLength*Math.cos(rotation);
  drawHand(cX, cY, endX, endY);
}

// draw Hand for hours
function drawHoursHand() {
  var rotationUnit = 5 * hours + minutes / 12;
  var rotationFactor = Math.PI / 30;
  var rotation = rotationUnit*rotationFactor;
  var handLength = 0.4*radius;

  endX = cX + handLength*Math.sin(rotation);
  endY = cY - handLength*Math.cos(rotation);
  drawHand(cX, cY, endX, endY);
}

function drawClockBackground() {
```

```
        var correction = 1/300;
        var shift_unit = 1/170;
        var shift_factor = 1/30;
        var angle_initial_position = 2;
        var angle_current_position_begin = 0;
        var angle_current_position_end = 0;
        var repeat = 60;
        var lineWidth = 10;

        for (var i=0; i < repeat; i+=1) {
          angle_current_position_begin = angle_initial_position -
            (i * shift_factor) - correction;
          angle_current_position_end =
            angle_current_position_begin + shift_unit;

          if (i % 5 == 0) lineWidth = 20;
          else lineWidth = 10;

          drawArcAtPosition(cX, cY, radius,
            angle_current_position_begin*Math.PI,
            angle_current_position_end*Math.PI, false, lineWidth);
        }
        drawLittleCircle(cX, cY);
      }

      function drawArcAtPosition(cX, cY, radius, start_angle,
        end_angle, counterclockwise, lineWidth) {
        canvasElement.beginPath();
        canvasElement.arc(cX, cY, radius, start_angle, end_angle,
          counterclockwise);
        canvasElement.lineWidth = lineWidth;
        canvasElement.strokeStyle = "black";
        canvasElement.stroke();
        canvasElement.closePath();
      }
      function drawLittleCircle(cX, cY) {
        drawArcAtPosition(cX, cY, 4, 0*Math.PI, 2*Math.PI, false,
          4);
      }

    </script>
  </head>
  <body onload="init()">
    <canvas id="myclock" height="500" width="500"></canvas>
  </body>
</html>
```

If you can see the output of your code as the following image, then congratulations! You successfully created your HTML clock using canvas:

Summary

In this chapter, we have learned the basics of HTML canvas. I hope that you can now draw anything using the HTML canvas. You may have played online games; the components of most of them are drawn using HTML canvas. Therefore, if you want to develop your own web applications or games, you need to learn about canvas. You can easily code to draw and animate the shapes using JavaScript.

In the next chapter, we will develop a game called **Rat-man** using the HTML canvas. Before starting *Chapter 8, Building Rat-man!*, I hope that you've learned a lot about HTML canvas through this chapter. If you've, let's develop our game now.

8
Building Rat-man!

In this chapter, we will be building a game called **Rat-man**, which is actually a modified version of the famous game **Pac-Man**. We will use canvas, JavaScript, CSS, and HTML to build our game.

Let's start with introducing our game's characters:

- Our game will have one rat. The player will act as the rat.
- There will be four cats who will try to catch the rat and a lot of cheese for the rat to eat.
- The main goal of the game is to eat all the cheese without being caught by the monster cats.

Sounds fun, right? Let's get right to it...

> To make our code clean, we will keep our JavaScript, CSS, and images files in separate folders. We will have three primary folders named as follows:
> - css
> - img
> - scripts

Game user interface

To start building our game, we need to prepare our canvas. Our HTML file should look similar to the following:

```
<html>
  <head>
  </head>
  <body>
    <canvas id="main_canvas"></canvas>
  </body>
</html>
```

Our game user interface will be in the <body></body> tags. We will add JavaScript to our canvas soon.

In the `css` folder, create a CSS file named `styles.css`, which will contain the following code for our HTML body, `canvas`, and a play `button`:

```
body {
  position: absolute;
  top: 0;
  right: 0;
  bottom: 0;
  left: 0;
  background-color: #ffffff;
  -webkit-background-size: cover;
  -moz-background-size: cover;
  -o-background-size: cover;
  background-size: cover;
  overflow: hidden;
}

canvas {
  position: absolute;
  top: 0;
  right: 0;
  bottom: 0;
  left: 0;
  margin: auto;
  border: 10px solid rgba(63, 72, 204, 0.7);
  border-radius: 20px;
  box-shadow: 0 0 500px 100px #ffffff;
}

button {
```

```
    width: 100%;
    height: 100%;
    background-color: #000000;
    color: #FFFFFF;
    font-size: 60px;
    opacity: 0;
    z-index: 1000;
    transition: 5s ease;
    visibility: hidden;
}
```

Create another CSS file named `reset.css` in the same folder and add the following code to the CSS file. This file will design the user interface for the initial screen of the game:

```
html, body, div, span, applet, object, iframe,
h1, h2, h3, h4, h5, h6, p, blockquote, pre,
a, abbr, acronym, address, big, cite, code,
del, dfn, em, img, ins, kbd, q, s, samp,
small, strike, strong, sub, sup, tt, var,
b, u, i, center,
dl, dt, dd, ol, ul, li,
fieldset, form, label, legend,
table, caption, tbody, tfoot, thead, tr, th, td,
article, aside, canvas, details, embed,
figure, figcaption, footer, header, hgroup,
menu, nav, output, ruby, section, summary,
time, mark, audio, video {
  margin: 0;
  padding: 0;
  border: 0;
  font-size: 100%;
  font: inherit;
  vertical-align: baseline;
}
article, aside, details, figcaption, figure,
footer, header, hgroup, menu, nav, section {
  display: block;
}

body {
  line-height: 0;
}

ol, ul {
```

```
      list-style: none;
    }

    blockquote, q {
      quotes: none;
    }

    blockquote:before, blockquote:after,
    q:before, q:after {
      content: '';
      content: none;
    }

    table {
      border-collapse: collapse;
      border-spacing: 0;
    }
```

Save both the files and include them in your HTML file with the following code in the <head></head> tags:

```
<link href="css/styles.css" rel="stylesheet"/>
<link href="css/reset.css" rel="stylesheet"/>
```

If you open an HTML file of a browser now, you will see the following image:

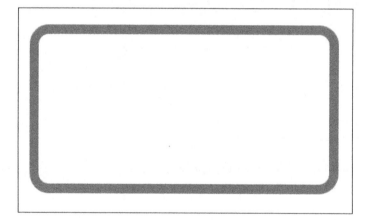

We are going to draw our game interface in the preceding rectangle.

Adding functionalities to the game

To add the user interface and the game's functionalities, we will be needing JavaScript. We will need the following JavaScript files in the `scripts` folder:

- `app.main.js`
- `app.display_functions.js`
- `app.init.js`
- `app.key_handler.js`
- `app.movement_functions.js`
- `app.constants.js`

The app.main.js file

Our `app.main.js` file should contain the following function that will deal with the `app.key_handler.js` file and your computer's keyboard. It will also call the `app.init.js` file for the initialization of our variables.

 Here we used `app.main.js`; You need not name your JavaScript file like this. But it is a good practice to maintain the naming convention.

The following code is the content of the `app.main.js` file:

```
(function () {
  "use strict";
  APP.Init();
  APP.timer = setInterval(APP.Show_World, 1000 / APP.GAME_FPS);
  window.addEventListener("keydown", APP.Keydown_Handler, false);
  APP.Reset = function () {
    APP.map.Init();
    APP.player.Init();
    APP.monsters.Init();
    APP.blackout.style.transition = "0s";
    APP.blackout.style.visibility = "hidden";
    setTimeout(function () {
      APP.timer = setInterval(APP.Show_World, 1000 /
        APP.GAME_FPS);
      APP.blackout.style.opacity = 0;
      APP.blackout.style.transition = "5s ease";
    }, 100);
  };
}());
```

The app.display_functions.js file

In our `app.display_functions.js` file, we will write a function, where we will include the `APP.Show_world` function, which is used in the `app.init.js` file.

The function should contain the following code (refer to the comments to understand what each step does):

```
APP.Show_World = function () {
  var i,
  dots = 0; //initialized cheese number
  dots = APP.map.Draw(); //put our cheese on the canvas
  if (!dots) {
    APP.Game_Over("YOU WIN!"); //if all cheese are ate by the
      rat, then the screen should display this.
  }
  */This loop is determine if the rat is caught by the cats  */
  for (i = 0; i < APP.MONSTERS_QUANTITY; i++) {
    if (APP.monsters[i].x === APP.player.x) {
      if (APP.monsters[i].y === APP.player.y) {
        APP.Game_Over("YOU LOSE!");
      }
    }
  }
  APP.monsters.Move(); //cats' movement function
  APP.player.Move();   // rat's movement function
  APP.player.Check_For_Dots(); //This function will check number
    of chees.
  APP.portals.Show(); //This will display two portals by using
    these the rat can escape.
  APP.player.Show(); //This will show the rat on the canvas.
    /* this function will show the monster on the canvas */
  for (i = 0; i < APP.MONSTERS_QUANTITY; i++) {
    APP.monsters[i].Show();
  }
};
```

The `APP.map.Draw` function will hold the following code:

```
APP.map.Draw = function () {
  var i, j, image, x, y, dot_counter = 0; //initialized
    variables.
  /*this loop will create our game map/maze */
  for (i = 0; i < APP.MAP_WIDTH; i++) {
    for (j = 0; j < APP.MAP_HEIGHT; j++) {
      image = APP.images[APP.map.cells[j][i]];
```

```
          x = i * APP.CELL_WIDTH;
          y = j * APP.CELL_HEIGHT;
          APP.context.drawImage(image, x, y);
          if (APP.map.cells[j][i] === APP.DOT_CELL_DIGIT) {
            dot_counter++;
          }
        }
      }
    }
    return dot_counter;
};
```

For the cats' movement, we will use the APP.monsters.Move function with the following code:

```
APP.monsters.Move = function () {
  var i;
  /*This loop will define the cats' quantity */
  for (i = 0; i < APP.MONSTERS_QUANTITY; i++) {
    if (APP.monsters[i].frame === APP.monsters[i].speed) {
      if (APP.monsters[i].direction !== APP.Direction.STOP) {
        APP.monsters[i].previus_direction =
        APP.monsters[i].direction;
      }
      APP.monsters[i].Select_Direction(); //Will select the
        cats' direction.
      APP.monsters[i].Check_Direction(); //Will check the
        cats' direction.
      APP.monsters[i].Check_Wall();//Will check the
        surroundings of the canvas or any block.
    }
    /* These conditions will check the boundaries of the
       canvas and make the cats move. */
    if (APP.monsters[i].direction !== APP.Direction.STOP) {
      if (APP.monsters[i].up) {
        APP.monsters[i].Move_Up();
      }
      if (APP.monsters[i].down) {
        APP.monsters[i].Move_Down();
      }
      if (APP.monsters[i].left) {
        APP.monsters[i].Move_Left();
      }
      if (APP.monsters[i].right) {
```

```
            APP.monsters[i].Move_Right();
        }
      }
    }
};
```

Our rat will move when the APP.player.Move() function is called with the following code:

```
APP.player.Move = function () {
  if (APP.player.frame === APP.player.speed) {
    APP.player.Check_Direction();
    APP.player.Check_Wall(); //This will check wall
  }
  /* these conditions will check our rat's valid movements */
  if (APP.player.direction !== APP.Direction.STOP) {
    if (APP.player.up) {
      APP.player.Move_Up();
    }
    if (APP.player.down) {
      APP.player.Move_Down();
    }
    if (APP.player.left) {
      APP.player.Move_Left();
    }
    if (APP.player.right) {
      APP.player.Move_Right();
    }
  }
};
/*this function will feed our rat the chees */
APP.player.Check_For_Dots = function () {
  if (APP.map.marks[APP.player.y][APP.player.x] ===
    APP.DOT_MARK) {
    APP.player.bonuses++;
    APP.map.marks[APP.player.y][APP.player.x] =
      APP.BLANK_MARK;
    APP.map.cells[APP.player.y][APP.player.x] =
      APP.BLANK_CELL_DIGIT;
  }
};
```

Now, we will make our rat visible on our canvas while moving the rat on the blocks by calling the function with the following code:

```
APP.player.Show = function () {
  //initializing our needed variables.
  var figure_offset = 5,
  frame_number = 2 - Math.floor(this.frame / 3),
  frame_offset = 1 - this.frame / this.speed,
  image, x, y;
  /* conditions for the rat's direction for up, down, left,
    right*/
  if (this.up) {
    image = this.up_images[frame_number];
    x = (this.x * APP.CELL_WIDTH) - figure_offset;
    y = ((this.y - frame_offset) * APP.CELL_HEIGHT) -
      figure_offset;

  } else if (this.down) {
    image = this.down_images[frame_number];
    x = (this.x * APP.CELL_WIDTH) - figure_offset;
    y = ((this.y + frame_offset) * APP.CELL_HEIGHT) -
      figure_offset;

  } else if (this.right) {
    image = this.right_images[frame_number];
    x = ((this.x + frame_offset) * APP.CELL_WIDTH) -
      figure_offset;
    y = (this.y * APP.CELL_HEIGHT) - figure_offset;

  } else {
    image = this.left_images[frame_number];
    x = ((this.x - frame_offset) * APP.CELL_WIDTH) -
      figure_offset;
    y = (this.y * APP.CELL_HEIGHT) - figure_offset;

  }
  APP.context.drawImage(image, x, y);
};
```

To show our cats on the canvas, we need to use the following code in our `APP.Show_Monster()` function:

```
APP.Show_Monster = function () {
  //initializing needed variables.
  var figure_offset = 15,
```

```
    frame_offset = 1 - this.frame / this.speed,
    image, x, y;
    /* binding the cats' directions for 4 directions*/
    if (this.up) {
      image = this.up_images[0];
      x = (this.x * APP.CELL_WIDTH) - figure_offset;
      y = ((this.y - frame_offset) * APP.CELL_HEIGHT) -
        figure_offset;

    } else if (this.down) {

      image = this.down_images[0];
      x = (this.x * APP.CELL_WIDTH) - figure_offset;
      y = ((this.y + frame_offset) * APP.CELL_HEIGHT) -
        figure_offset;

    } else if (this.right) {

      image = this.right_images[0];
      x = ((this.x + frame_offset) * APP.CELL_WIDTH) -
        figure_offset;
      y = (this.y * APP.CELL_HEIGHT) - figure_offset;

    } else {

      image = this.left_images[0];
      x = ((this.x - frame_offset) * APP.CELL_WIDTH) -
        figure_offset;
      y = (this.y * APP.CELL_HEIGHT) - figure_offset;

    }

    APP.context.drawImage(image, x, y);
  };
```

To show the portal, we need to write another function called `APP.portals.Show ()`, including the following code:

```
    APP.portals.Show = function () {
      //initialized variables and incremented.
      var offset, frame_offset, sw = +!this.raise;
      frame_offset = sw - this.frame_counter / (this.speed *
        APP.GAME_FPS);
      /*controlled frame of the game */
      offset = Math.abs(this.width * frame_offset);
```

```
   APP.context.drawImage(this[0].image, this[0].x - offset,
     this[0].y);
   APP.context.drawImage(this[1].image, this[1].x + offset,
     this[1].y);
   this.frame_counter++;
   if (this.frame_counter === this.speed * APP.GAME_FPS) {
     this.frame_counter = 0;
     this.raise = !this.raise;
   }
 };
```

The user will need to see a message after the game is over or make the screen blur. To do this, we need to declare another function called APP.Game_Over() with the following code:

```
   APP.Game_Over = function (condition) {
     clearInterval(APP.timer);
     APP.blackout = document.getElementById("blackout");
     APP.blackout.textContent = condition;
     APP.blackout.style.visibility = "visible";
     APP.blackout.style.opacity = 0.7;
   };
```

The app.init.js file

Our app.init.js file will contain a function. In the function, we will declare the following variables:

```
   APP.map = {};
   APP.player = {};
   APP.monsters = [{}, {}, {}, {}];
   APP.portals = [{}, {}];
   APP.images = [];
   APP.timer = {};
   APP.canvas = {};
   APP.context = {};
   APP.blackout = document.getElementById("blackout");
```

Write a function that will contain few more variables, as follows:

```
   APP.Init = function () {
     APP.map.Init();
     APP.player.Init();
     APP.portals.Init();
```

```
        APP.monsters.Init();
        APP.images.Init();
        APP.canvas.Init();
    };
```

Now, we will initialize our game's map:

```
APP.map.Init = function () {

    //initializing few variables ; few of them may look ugly, but
        don't worry they are a little bit random.
    var i, j, map_in_strings = [
                "50000000000002500000000000002",
                "17777777777711777777777777771",
                "17500275000271175000275002711",
                "17166171666171171666171666171",
                "17400374000374374000374000371",
                "17777777777777777777777777771",
                "17500275275000000275275002711",
                "17400371174002500371174003711",
                "17777771177771177777117777771",
                "40000271400261165003175000003",
                "00002171500364364002171500000",
                "66661171166666666666117116666",
                "00003171165026650261171400000",
                "00000374361536642164374000000",
                "66666667666116666116667666666",
                "00000275261400003165275000000",
                "00002171164000000361171500000",
                "66661171166666666666117116666",
                "00003171165000000261171400000",
                "50000374364002500364374000002",
                "17777777777711777777777777771",
                "17500275000271175000275002711",
                "17402174000374374000371503711",
                "17771177777777777777117117771",
                "40271175275000000027527117503",
                "50374371174002500371174374402",
                "17777771177771177777117777771",
                "17500003400271175003400000271",
                "17400000000374374000000000371",
                "17777777777777777777777777771",
                "40000000000000000000000000003"
            ];
```

```
      APP.map.cells = [];
      for (i = 0; i < APP.MAP_HEIGHT; i++) {
        APP.map.cells[i] = [];
        for (j = 0; j < APP.MAP_WIDTH; j++) {
          APP.map.cells[i][j] = +map_in_strings[i].charAt(j);
        }
      }
      APP.map.marks = [];
      /* This loop will determine the map's size */
      for (i = 0; i < APP.MAP_HEIGHT; i++) {
        APP.map.marks[i] = [];
        for (j = 0; j < APP.MAP_WIDTH; j++) {
          if (APP.map.cells[i][j] <= APP.WALL_CELL_DIGIT) {
            APP.map.marks[i][j] = APP.WALL_MARK;
          } else if (APP.map.cells[i][j] === APP.BLANK_CELL_DIGIT) {
            APP.map.marks[i][j] = APP.BLANK_MARK;
          } else if (APP.map.cells[i][j] === APP.DOT_CELL_DIGIT) {
            APP.map.marks[i][j] = APP.DOT_MARK;
          }
        }
      }
    };
```

Images for Rat-man!

To build the game, we will need a few images. We will keep all our images in the img folder. In the img folder, we will create four folders, as shown in the following:

- monsters
- player
- portal
- walls

We will keep two images, named dot.png and blank.png, in the img folder.

The monsters folder

In the `monsters` folder, create four folders with our cats' names.

Say that our cats' names are as follows (you can name them whatever you want):

- blinky
- inky
- pinky
- clyde

Each cat folder will have four folders for the directed images of the cats. The folder names are as follows:

- up
- down
- left
- right

Each direction folder should contain an image of our cat. The image name should be `0.png`.

You need to keep your image 50 x 50 px.

The player folder

The `player` folder should contain four folders for the direction of our rat. The folders should be named as shown in the following:

- up
- down
- left
- right

Each folder should contain the rat's directed image. There need to be two images, `0.png` and `1.png`. One image is the open mouthed rat and another is of the closed mouthed rat. The images need to be 50 x 50 px.

The portal folder

The `portal` folder should contain two images of the portal through which our rat will travel from one end to another. The images names should be `0.png` and `1.png`.

The walls folder

The `walls` folder should have five images to draw the walls in the canvas.

The images should be named `0.png`, `1.png`, `2.png`, `3.png`, and `4.png`. The images will be the corners and straight lines of the wall.

The hierarchical representation of the images used in building our game is as follows:

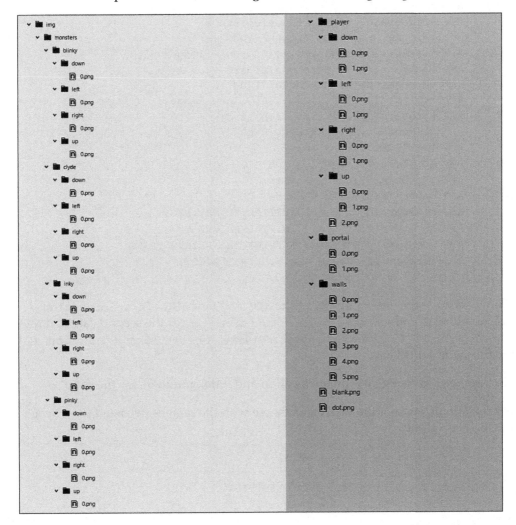

Adding images to our cats

We will write four functions to add perfect images for our cats. The function should look similar to the following function:

```
APP.monsters[0].Init = function () {
  APP.monsters[0].up_images = [];
  APP.monsters[0].right_images = [];
  APP.monsters[0].down_images = [];
  APP.monsters[0].left_images = [];
  APP.monsters[0].up_images[0] = new Image();
  APP.monsters[0].up_images[0].src =
    "img/monsters/blinky/up/0.png";
  APP.monsters[0].right_images[0] = new Image();
  APP.monsters[0].right_images[0].src =
    "img/monsters/blinky/right/0.png";
  APP.monsters[0].down_images[0] = new Image();
  APP.monsters[0].down_images[0].src =
    "img/monsters/blinky/down/0.png";
  APP.monsters[0].left_images[0] = new Image();
  APP.monsters[0].left_images[0].src =
    "img/monsters/blinky/left/0.png";
  APP.monsters[0].up = false;
  APP.monsters[0].right = true;
  APP.monsters[0].down = false;
  APP.monsters[0].left = false;
  APP.monsters[0].x = APP.INITIAL_BLINKY_X;
  APP.monsters[0].y = APP.INITIAL_BLINKY_Y;
  APP.monsters[0].frame = APP.INITIAL_BLINKY_FRAME;
  APP.monsters[0].speed = APP.BLINKY_SPEED;
};
```

We will change the index number of the `APP.monsters[0].Init = function ();` function to `APP.monsters[1].Init = function ();` for the second cat. And `APP.monsters[2].Init = function ()` & `APP.monsters[3].Init = function ()` for the third and fourth cats.

We also need to change the image location and index numbers for the cats.

For the initialization of the walls and cheese with the images, we need to write a function, as follows:

```
APP.images.Init = function () {
  var i;
  for (i = 0; i <= APP.DOT_CELL_DIGIT; i++) {
    APP.images[i] = new Image();
```

```
    }
    APP.images[0].src = "img/walls/0.png";
    APP.images[1].src = "img/walls/1.png";
    APP.images[2].src = "img/walls/2.png";
    APP.images[3].src = "img/walls/3.png";
    APP.images[4].src = "img/walls/4.png";
    APP.images[5].src = "img/walls/5.png";
    APP.images[6].src = "img/blank.png";
    APP.images[7].src = "img/dot.png";
};
```

Draw the canvas

We will draw our canvas by adding the following function to our `app.init.js` file:

```
APP.canvas.Init = function () {
    APP.canvas = document.getElementById("main_canvas");
    APP.canvas.width = APP.MAP_WIDTH * APP.CELL_WIDTH;
    APP.canvas.height = APP.MAP_HEIGHT * APP.CELL_HEIGHT;
    APP.context = APP.canvas.getContext("2d");
    APP.context.fillStyle = APP.BG_COLOR;
    APP.context.fillRect(0, 0, APP.canvas.width, APP.canvas.height);
};
```

The app.key_handler.js file

Now, in the `app.key_handler.js` file, we will write our code to give the player the ability to move our rat using the keyboard. The code should look similar to the following:

```
APP.Keydown_Handler = function (event) {
    "use strict";
    var KEYS = {
        /* We will initialize the arrow keys first. 37 = left key, 38
          = up key, 39 = right key and 40 = down key. */
        LEFT    : 37,
        UP      : 38,
        RIGHT   : 39,
        DOWN    : 40
    };
    /* This switch-case will handle the key pressing and the rat's
      movement. */
    switch (event.keyCode) {
```

```
      case KEYS.UP:
        APP.player.direction = APP.Direction.UP;
        break;
      case KEYS.RIGHT:
        APP.player.direction = APP.Direction.RIGHT;
        break;
      case KEYS.DOWN:
        APP.player.direction = APP.Direction.DOWN;
        break;
      case KEYS.LEFT:
        APP.player.direction = APP.Direction.LEFT;
        break;
    }
};
```

The app.movement_functions.js file

We need to take a look where our wall ends or starts while pressing the keys. We
need to stop moving the rat when we reach the edges. Therefore, we have to set
some conditions for that. The first one is to check the direction. The function can be
written as shown in the following:

```
APP.Check_Direction = function () {
  switch (this.direction) {
    case APP.Direction.UP:
      if (APP.map.marks[this.y - 1][this.x] !== APP.WALL_MARK){
        this.up = true;
        this.down = false;
        this.right = false;
        this.left = false;
        return true;
      }
      break;
    case APP.Direction.DOWN:
      if (APP.map.marks[this.y + 1][this.x] !== APP.WALL_MARK) {
        this.up = false;
        this.down = true;
        this.right = false;
        this.left = false;
        return true;
      }
      break;
    case APP.Direction.RIGHT:
      if (APP.map.marks[this.y][this.x + 1] !== APP.WALL_MARK) {
```

```
            this.up = false;
            this.down = false;
            this.right = true;
            this.left = false;
            return true;
          }
          break;
        case APP.Direction.LEFT:
          if (APP.map.marks[this.y][this.x - 1] !== APP.WALL_MARK) {
            this.up = false;
            this.down = false;
            this.right = false;
            this.left = true;
            return true;
          }
          break;
      }
      return false;
    };
```

While checking the directions, we also need to move in the right direction. The function to select the direction can be written as follows:

```
APP.Select_Direction = function () {
  var possible_directions = [],
  direction_quantity = 9,
  rnd;
  switch (this.previus_direction) {
    case APP.Direction.UP:
      possible_directions[0] = APP.Direction.UP;
      possible_directions[1] = APP.Direction.UP;
      possible_directions[2] = APP.Direction.UP;
      possible_directions[3] = APP.Direction.UP;
      possible_directions[4] = APP.Direction.UP;
      possible_directions[5] = APP.Direction.UP;
      possible_directions[6] = APP.Direction.RIGHT;
      possible_directions[7] = APP.Direction.DOWN;
      possible_directions[8] = APP.Direction.LEFT;
      break;
    case APP.Direction.RIGHT:
      possible_directions[0] = APP.Direction.RIGHT;
      possible_directions[1] = APP.Direction.RIGHT;
      possible_directions[2] = APP.Direction.RIGHT;
      possible_directions[3] = APP.Direction.RIGHT;
      possible_directions[4] = APP.Direction.RIGHT;
```

```
        possible_directions[5] = APP.Direction.RIGHT;
        possible_directions[6] = APP.Direction.UP;
        possible_directions[7] = APP.Direction.DOWN;
        possible_directions[8] = APP.Direction.LEFT;
        break;
      case APP.Direction.DOWN:
        possible_directions[0] = APP.Direction.DOWN;
        possible_directions[1] = APP.Direction.DOWN;
        possible_directions[2] = APP.Direction.DOWN;
        possible_directions[3] = APP.Direction.DOWN;
        possible_directions[4] = APP.Direction.DOWN;
        possible_directions[5] = APP.Direction.DOWN;
        possible_directions[6] = APP.Direction.UP;
        possible_directions[7] = APP.Direction.RIGHT;
        possible_directions[8] = APP.Direction.LEFT;
        break;
      case APP.Direction.LEFT:
        possible_directions[0] = APP.Direction.LEFT;
        possible_directions[1] = APP.Direction.LEFT;
        possible_directions[2] = APP.Direction.LEFT;
        possible_directions[3] = APP.Direction.LEFT;
        possible_directions[4] = APP.Direction.LEFT;
        possible_directions[5] = APP.Direction.LEFT;
        possible_directions[6] = APP.Direction.UP;
        possible_directions[7] = APP.Direction.RIGHT;
        possible_directions[8] = APP.Direction.DOWN;
        break;
    }
    rnd = Math.floor(Math.random() * direction_quantity);
    this.direction = possible_directions[rnd];
  };
```

Now, we have to check for the walls. We can do this by adding a few conditions to the function as shown in the following:

```
APP.Check_Wall = function () {
  if (this.up) {
    if (APP.map.marks[this.y - 1][this.x] !== APP.WALL_MARK) {
      this.up = true;
      this.down = false;
      this.right = false;
      this.left = false;
    } else {
      this.direction = APP.Direction.STOP;
    }
```

```
      }

  if (this.right) {
    if (APP.map.marks[this.y][this.x + 1] !== APP.WALL_MARK) {
      this.up = false;
      this.down = false;
      this.right = true;
      this.left = false;
    } else {
      this.direction = APP.Direction.STOP;
    }
  }

  if (this.down) {
    if (APP.map.marks[this.y + 1][this.x] !== APP.WALL_MARK) {
      this.up = false;
      this.down = true;
      this.right = false;
      this.left = false;
    } else {
      this.direction = APP.Direction.STOP;
    }
  }

  if (this.left) {
    if (APP.map.marks[this.y][this.x - 1] !== APP.WALL_MARK) {
      this.up = false;
      this.down = false;
      this.right = false;
      this.left = true;
    } else {
      this.direction = APP.Direction.STOP;
    }
  }
};
```

The movement of the arrow keys should be well defined. We should create the
following functions for the arrow keys:

```
APP.Move_Up = function () {
  if (this.frame === 0) {
    this.frame = this.speed;
    this.y--;
  } else {
```

```
        this.frame--;
      }
    if (this.y < 0) {
      this.y = APP.MAP_HEIGHT - 1;
    }
  };
  APP.Move_Right = function () {
    if (this.frame === 0) {
      this.frame = this.speed;
      this.x++;
    } else {
      this.frame--;
    }
    if (this.x >= APP.MAP_WIDTH) {
      this.x = 0;
    }
  };
  APP.Move_Down = function () {
    if (this.frame === 0) {
      this.frame = this.speed;
      this.y++;
    } else {
      this.frame--;
    }
    if (this.y >= APP.MAP_HEIGHT) {
      this.y = 0;
    }
  };
  APP.Move_Left = function () {
    if (this.frame === 0) {
      this.frame = this.speed;
      this.x--;
    } else {
      this.frame--;
    }
    if (this.x < 0) {
      this.x = APP.MAP_WIDTH - 1;
    }
  };
```

The app.constants.js file

To keep our game's canvas clean and in good shape, we need to initialize a few variables with a few fixed variables (for example, height of map, height of cell, width of map, width of cell, and so on). We can do this by writing the following code in our `app.constants.js` file. Check the comments with the code to get a clear idea how the code will work:

```javascript
var APP = {};
(function () {
  "use strict";
  //used for map's size and each cell's size
  APP.MAP_WIDTH = 28;
  APP.MAP_HEIGHT = 31;
  APP.CELL_WIDTH = 20;
  APP.CELL_HEIGHT = 20;
  APP.BG_COLOR = "#000000";
  APP.GAME_FPS = 40;
  APP.PLAYER_SPEED = 8;
  APP.INITIAL_PLAYER_FRAME = 8;
  APP.INITIAL_PLAYER_X = 14;
  APP.INITIAL_PLAYER_Y = 23;
  APP.WALL_CELL_DIGIT = 5;
  APP.BLANK_CELL_DIGIT = 6;
  APP.DOT_CELL_DIGIT = 7;
  APP.WALL_MARK = "W";
  APP.BLANK_MARK = "B";
  APP.DOT_MARK = "D";
  APP.PORTAL_BLINKING_SPEED = 2;
  APP.PORTAL_WIDTH = 20;
  APP.FIRST_PORTAL_X = 0;
  APP.FIRST_PORTAL_Y = 265;
  APP.SECOND_PORTAL_X = 510;
  APP.SECOND_PORTAL_Y = 265;
  APP.MONSTERS_QUANTITY = 4;
  APP.INKY_SPEED = 7;
  //for the cat's speed and position.
  APP.INITIAL_INKY_X = 12;
  APP.INITIAL_INKY_Y = 14;
  APP.INITIAL_INKY_FRAME = 7;
  APP.PINKY_SPEED = 7;
  APP.INITIAL_PINKY_X = 13;
  APP.INITIAL_PINKY_Y = 14;
  APP.INITIAL_PINKY_FRAME = 4;
```

```
        APP.BLINKY_SPEED = 7;
        APP.INITIAL_BLINKY_X = 14;
        APP.INITIAL_BLINKY_Y = 11;
        APP.INITIAL_BLINKY_FRAME = 4;
        APP.CLYDE_SPEED = 7;
        APP.INITIAL_CLYDE_X = 15;
        APP.INITIAL_CLYDE_Y = 14;
        APP.INITIAL_CLYDE_FRAME = 7;
        APP.Direction = {
          UP      : "UP",
          RIGHT   : "RIGHT",
          DOWN    : "DOWN",
          LEFT    : "LEFT",
          STOP    : "STOP"
        };
    }) ();
```

Playing the game

If you correctly integrated the code and your HTML file now looks similar to the
following, you can now run the HTML file:

```html
<html>
  <head>
    <link href="css/reset.css" rel="stylesheet"/>
    <link href="css/styles.css" rel="stylesheet"/>
  </head>
  <body>
    <canvas id="main_canvas"></canvas>
    <button id="blackout" onclick="APP.Reset()"></button>
    <script src="scripts/app.constants.js"></script>
    <script src="scripts/app.init.js"></script>
    <script src="scripts/app.display_functions.js"></script>
    <script src="scripts/app.movement_functions.js"></script>
    <script src="scripts/app.key_handler.js"></script>
    <script src="scripts/app.main.js"></script>
  </body>
</html>
```

After running the HTML file on your browser, you will be able to see the following screen:

Congratulations! You have successfully built Rat-man!

To play the game, click anywhere on the canvas and use the arrow keys for your rat's movement.

If you lose all your lives, you will see the following screen:

If you win, you will see the following screen:

Summary

We have built the Rat-man! I hope that you are now playing the game that you have
built. If you cannot play the game after coding for hours, don't worry. Keep calm and
try again. The whole source code and required images are included in the book. You
can download and run it. However, before doing this, I would suggest you to try at
least twice. Let's move on to *Chapter 9, Tidying up Your Code Using OOP*, for a better
idea about making files or folders and accessing them.

9
Tidying up Your Code Using OOP

In this chapter, we are going to learn about **object-oriented programming** (OOP) and discuss the code of the famous game, **Hangman**.

"OOP is a programming paradigm that uses abstraction to create models based on the real world. OOP uses several techniques from previously established paradigms, including modularity, polymorphism, and encapsulation." or "OOP languages typically are identified through their use of classes to create multiple objects that have the same properties and methods."

You probably have assumed that JavaScript is an object-oriented programming language. Yes, you are absolutely correct. Let's see why it is an OOP language. If a computer programming language has the following few features, we call it object oriented:

- Inheritance
- Polymorphism
- Encapsulation
- Abstraction

Before going any further, let's discuss **objects**. We create objects in JavaScript in the following manner:

```
var person = new Object();
person.name = "Harry Potter";
person.age = 22;
person.job = "Magician";
```

We created an object for a person. We added few properties of person.

If we want to access any of the property of the object, we need to call the property.

Consider that you want to have a popup of the `name` property of the preceding `person` object. You can do this with the following method:

```
person.callName = function(){
    alert(this.name);
};
```

We can write the preceding code as shown in the following:

```
var person = {
    name: "Harry Potter",
    age: 22,
    job: "Magician",
    callName: function(){
    alert(this.name);
    }
};
```

Inheritance in JavaScript

To inherit means derive something (such as, characteristics, quality, and so on) from one's parents or ancestors. In programming languages, when a class or object is based on another class or object in order to maintain the same behavior of the parent class or object is known as **inheritance**.

We can also say that this is a concept of gaining properties or behaviors of something else.

Suppose, X inherits something from Y; it is like X is a type of Y.

JavaScript occupies the inheritance capability. Let's take a look at an example. A bird inherits from an animal as a bird is a type of animal. Therefore, a bird can do the same thing that an animal does.

This kind of relationship in JavaScript is a little complex and needs a syntax. We need to use a special object called `prototype`, which assigns the properties to a type. We need to remember that only function has prototypes. Our `Animal` function should look similar to the following:

```
function Animal(){
//We can code here.
};
```

To add a few properties of the function, we need to add a prototype as shown in the following:

```
Animal.prototype.eat = function(){
  alert("Animal can eat.");
};
```

Let's create prototypes for our `Bird` function. Our function and prototypes should look similar to the following:

```
function Bird(){
};
Bird.prototype = new Animal();
Bird.prototype.fly = function(){
  alert("Birds can fly.");
};
Bird.prototype.sing = function(){
  alert("Bird can sing.");
};
```

The result of the prototypes and function is that any `Bird` that you create will have the properties of `Animal` and `Bird`. However, if you create `Animal`, this will only have the properties of `Animal`. The properties of `Animal` are inherited by `Bird`.

Therefore, we can say that JavaScript has inheritance property.

Encapsulation in JavaScript

In OOP, **encapsulation** is one of the most important concepts that allows an object to group the members of public and private classes under a single name. We use encapsulation to protect our classes against accidental or willful folly. Encapsulation means to enclose something in or as if something is in a capsule.

Now, we will see whether JavaScript supports encapsulation. If it does, we can say that JavaScript is an OOP language. Let's take a look at the following example:

```
var person = {
  "name" : "Harry Potter",
  "age" : 22,
};
alert(person.name);
person.name = "John";
alert(person.name);
```

If we run this on the console. The first alert box will print the following image:

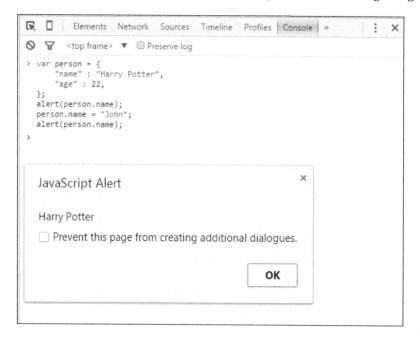

We changed the variable name to John. Therefore, the second alert box will be similar to the following image:

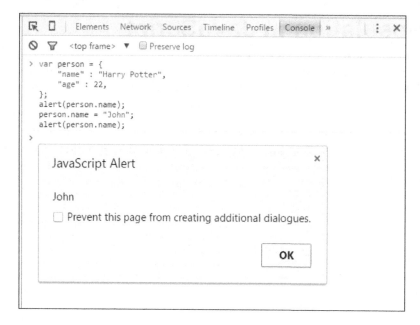

What would happen if we accidently assigned a number to the name variable?

Assigning a number to the name variable is perfectly acceptable. As far as JavaScript is concerned, a variable can accept any type of data as its value. However, we don't want a number in the place of a name. What do we do? We can use JavaScript's encapsulation property, as follows:

```
var person = function () {
  var Name = "Harry Potter";
  var reg = new RegExp(/\d+/);
  return {
    "setName" : function (newValue) {
      if ( reg.test(newValue) ) {
        alert("Invalid Name");
      }
      else {
        Name = newValue;
      }
    },
    "getName" : function () {
      return Name;
    }
  };
}();

alert(person.getName());   // Harry potter
person.setName( "John" );
alert(person.getName());   // John
person.setName( 42 ); // Invalid Name; the name is not changed.
person.Name = 42;       // Doesn't affect the private Name variable.
alert(person.getName());  // John is printed again.
```

Now, if we run the above code on console, the first output will show a popup with **Harry Potter** as we only called the `getName()` function. The `getName()` function has an initial value, which is `Harry Potter`:

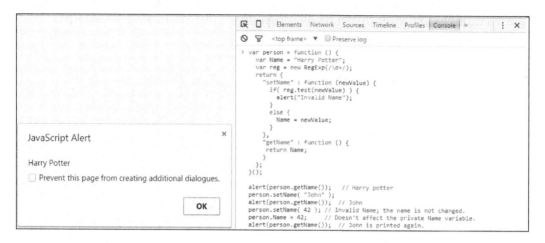

The second output will be as follows as we changed the `Name` property of `person` to `John` and again called the `getName()` function:

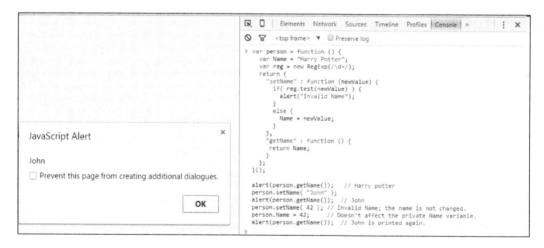

The third output will be as shown in the following as we tried to push a number to a string variable. A name cannot be an integer, therefore, **Invalid Name** popped up as we had a condition under the `if` statement:

The fourth output will be as shown in the following as the number was not added to the person's `Name` property. Therefore, we will get the last data that we pushed to the `Name` property:

We can now confirm that JavaScript supports encapsulation.

JavaScript also supports **polymorphism** and **abstraction**. If you would like to read about them, you can refer to the following link:

```
https://developer.mozilla.org/en-US/docs/Web/JavaScript/Introduction_
to_Object-Oriented_JavaScript
```

Let's do something fun. You may have heard of the game called Hangman. We'll discuss the OOP in that game. First, let's introduce you to the game.

The player needs to guess a word. If he can guess the word correctly, he is safe; otherwise, he will be hanged. Take a look at the following image to get the clear idea about the game, as follows:

Dissecting Hangman

There are two folders and an HTML file for the Hangman game. The two folders are named as `css` and `js`. The `index.html` HTML file should contain the following code:

```html
<html lang="en" ng-app="hangman">
  <head>
    <title>Hangman</title>
    <link rel="stylesheet" href="css/styles.css">
    <script src="js/angular.min.js"></script>
  </head>
  <body ng-controller="StartHangman">
    <p>Hangman</p>
    <svg width="400" height="400">
      <rect ng-show="failedGuess.length >= 1" x="0" y="0"
        width="40" height="400"></rect>
      <rect ng-show="failedGuess.length >= 2" x="40" y="20"
        width="200" height="40"></rect>
      <rect ng-show="failedGuess.length >= 3" x="173" y="50"
        width="4" height="100"></rect>
      <circle ng-show="failedGuess.length >= 3" cx="175" cy="120"
        r="40"></circle>
      <line ng-show="failedGuess.length >= 4" x1="175" y1="150"
        x2="175" y2="185" style="stroke:rgb(0,0,0)"
        stroke-width="10"></line>
      <line ng-show="failedGuess.length >= 4" x1="175" y1="180"
        x2="100" y2="240" style="stroke:rgb(0,0,0)"
        stroke-width="10"></line>
      <line ng-show="failedGuess.length >= 5" x1="175" y1="180"
        x2="250" y2="240" style="stroke:rgb(0,0,0)"
        stroke-width="10"></line>
      <line ng-show="failedGuess.length >= 6" x1="175" y1="180"
        x2="175" y2="265" style="stroke:rgb(0,0,0)"
        stroke-width="10"></line>
      <line ng-show="failedGuess.length >= 7" x1="175" y1="260"
        x2="120" y2="340" style="stroke:rgb(0,0,0)"
        stroke-width="10"></line>
      <line ng-show="failedGuess.length >= 8" x1="175" y1="260"
        x2="230" y2="340" style="stroke:rgb(0,0,0)"
        stroke-width="10"></line>
    </svg>

    <div ng-show="stage == 'initial'">
      <h2>Please enter your secret words:</h2>
      <input type="text" ng-model="secretWords" autofocus
        ng-keyup="$event.keyCode == 13 ? startGame() : null">
```

```
        <button ng-click="startGame()">Enter</button>
    </div>

    <div ng-show="stage == 'play'">
      <h1>{{ answer }}</h1>
      <h2>Failed guess ({{ failedGuess.length }}) =
        {{ failedGuess}}</h2>

      <input type="text" ng-model="charGuess" id="char-guess"
        ng-keyup="$event.keyCode == 13 ? guess(charGuess) : null"
        placeholder="Guess a letter">
      <button ng-click="guess(charGuess)">Enter</button>
    </div>

    <div ng-show="stage == 'won'">
      <h1>You Win! :)</h1>
      <h2>That's right, the secret words is {{ secretWords }}</h2>
      <p>Press F5 to replay</p>
    </div>

    <div ng-show="stage == 'lost'">
      <h1>You Lose! :(</h1>
      <h2>The secret word is {{ secretWords }}</h2>
      <p>Press F5 to replay</p>
    </div>

    <script src="js/hangman.js"></script>
  </body>
</html>
```

The css folder should have a styles.css file. The styles.css file should contain the following code:

```
body {
  font-family: monospace;
  text-align: center;
  font-size: 16px;
  line-height: 1.40;
}

input[type="text"] {
  padding: 5px;
  font-family: monospace;
  height: 30px;
  font-size: 1.8em;
```

```
      background-color: #fff;
      border: 2px solid #000;
      vertical-align: bottom;
    }

    svg {
      margin: 0 0 30px;
    }

    button {
      cursor: pointer;
      margin: 0;
      height: 44px;
      background-color: #fff;
      border: 2px solid #000;
    }
```

There should be two JavaScript files in the `js` folder, `angular.min.js` and `hangman.js`.

The `angular.min.js` file is a framework. You can download it from `https://angularjs.org/` or it is available with the code bundle of the book.

The `hangman.js` file should have the following code:

```
var hangman = angular.module('hangman', []).controller(
  'StartHangman', StartHangman);
  function StartHangman($scope, $document) {
    $scope.stage = "initial";
    $scope.secretWords = "";
    $scope.answer = "";
    $scope.failedGuess = [];
    var hasWon = function() {
      var foundDash = $scope.answer.search(/-/);
      return (foundDash == -1);
    }
    var hasLost = function() {
      return ($scope.failedGuess.length >= 8);
    }
    $scope.startGame = function() {
      $scope.secretWords = $scope.secretWords.toLowerCase();
      for(i in $scope.secretWords) {
        $scope.answer += $scope.secretWords[i] == ' ' ? ' ' : '-';
      }
      $scope.stage = "play"
```

```
        }
        $scope.guess = function(ch) {
          ch = ch.toLowerCase();
          $scope.charGuess = "";
          if(ch.length != 1) {
            if(ch.length > 1) {
              alert("Please only enter one character at a time");
            }
          return ;
        }
        /* If ch is already in the failed guess list */
        for(i in $scope.failedGuess) {
          if(ch == $scope.failedGuess[i]) return ;
        }
        /* Check if it's part of the answer */
        var found = false;
        $scope.answer = $scope.answer.split(""); /* convert to array
          of char */
        for(i in $scope.secretWords) {
          if($scope.secretWords[i] === ch) {
            found = true;
            $scope.answer[i] = ch;
          }
        }
        $scope.answer = $scope.answer.join(""); /* convert back to
          string */
        if(!found) {
          $scope.failedGuess.push(ch);
        }
        if(hasWon()) {
          $scope.stage = "won";
        }
        if(hasLost()) {
          $scope.stage = "lost";
        }
      }
    }
```

Let's discuss the code.

We used `var hangman = angular.module('hangman', []).controller('StartHangman', StartHangman);` to import our `angular.min.js` file and start controlling the rest of our game's code.

We wrote a `StartHangman($scope, $document) {}` function, where we will write our code. We passed two variables, `$scope` and `$document`, from our `angular.min.js` file.

We initialized few variables, as follows:

```
$scope.stage = "initial";
$scope.secretWords = "";
$scope.answer = "";
$scope.failedGuess = [];
```

We wrote two functions for winning and losing the game, as follows:

```
var hasWon = function() {
  var foundDash = $scope.answer.search(/-/);
  return (foundDash == -1);
}
var hasLost = function() {
  return ($scope.failedGuess.length >= 8);
}
```

We have fixed our number of guesses here. Then, we wrote a function to start our game. We made an object and used the inheritance property of JavaScript, as shown in the following:

```
$scope.startGame = function() {
  $scope.secretWords = $scope.secretWords.toLowerCase();
  for(i in $scope.secretWords) {
    $scope.answer += $scope.secretWords[i] == ' ' ? ' ' : '-';
  }
  $scope.stage = "play"
}
```

We took an input from the player in order to store as our secret word.

The prompt page of the game will look similar to the following image:

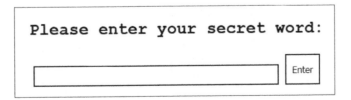

Then, our most important function, `$scope.guess = function(ch){}`, was introduced. We passed a character to the function and checked whether it matches any letters entered by the player with the secret word.

Summary

In this chapter, you learned the characteristics of an OOP language. We also saw the uses of the OOP characteristics in the famous game, Hangman! I hope you enjoyed creating and playing Hangman. We will see the possibilities of JavaScript in the next and final chapter of this book.

10
Possibilities

Throughout this book, we have explored a lot of topics related to JavaScript. You learned how to play with console; solve problems with JavaScript, HTML tags, CSS properties, and control statement; use jQuery; draw with canvas; build projects; and so on. However, have you ever thought about the opportunities that you got by reading the book and learning JavaScript?

Well, in this chapter, we are going to see why learning JavaScript is important and what are the fields of JavaScript.

JavaScript as your first programming language

JavaScript is the easiest language to start learning. It does not need any software to run. A modern browser and notepad are enough to start coding in JavaScript. JavaScript has some of the best online learning materials.

Websites such as Codecademy (`https://www.codecademy.com`), Code School (`https://www.codeschool.com`), CodePen (`http://codepen.io`), JS Bin (`https://jsbin.com`), and JSFiddle (`https://jsfiddle.net`) will help you learn JavaScript in short time.

JavaScript is everywhere

JavaScript is the only language that runs in almost every browser; even in smartphone browsers. As the web is everywhere, JavaScript is also everywhere.

JavaScript developer as profession

If you enjoy programming and want to build your career with programming, JavaScript is one of the best languages for this. I can say it would be difficult to make better choice than JavaScript. If you look at some of the trends in web development, you will see that real-time websites are like desktop applications. Heavy user interactions on websites such as dragging and dropping, audio and video interactions, and visualization of data are common nowadays. All of these are mostly done using JavaScript. Without JavaScript, we would not get the cool web applications (Google Map, Google Earth, Gmail, Facebook, and so on). JavaScript has made everything possible. No other language is as strong as JavaScript when you want to build web applications. The present world is web-based and web is powered by JavaScript in order to make it beautiful, dynamic, and secure. Therefore, choosing JavaScript with HTML and CSS as your future profession will be one of the best decisions in your life. The developers are known as frontend or full-stack developers.

All chores can be done by JavaScript

With JavaScript, you can do a lot of awesome things. From robotics to web app developing, JavaScript is a strong tool. Let's see how people use JavaScript in their tech life:

- Robotics
- 3D games
- Making apps for your smartphones
- Running web servers
- Running Ruby and Python
- Writing OS independent desktop applications
- Web scraping and screenshotting
- Web analytics
- Responsive and interactive contents
- Animation
- Creating cookies

Robotics

In robotics, you need to control your robot with logics. In real world, the logics are handled by microcontrollers. You may have heard of **Arduino**, an open source hardware that deals with microelectronics. Basically, Arduino controls microcontrollers using C code. However, if you know JavaScript, you can also code for it; to work with microprocessor/microcontroller and make your first robot. You can get help from `http://nodebots.io/` in order to see how JavaScript is used to build robots. Following is an image of Arduino UNO board:

An Arduino UNO

3D games

We have built and developed 2D games in this book. However, trust me, you can also build awesome 3D games with JavaScript. You can even play them via your favorite gamepad. To play with your gamepad, you need to use a gamepad API (`https://wiki.mozilla.org/GamepadAPI`).

You can play few online 3D games build with JavaScript at the following URL: `http://www.babylonjs.com/`.

Making apps for your smartphones

Have you ever thought of building an app for your smartphone? You can build apps for your smartphones with JavaScript. There are different types of platforms for smartphones (for example, Android, iOS, Tizen, Firefox OS, and so on). Every platform has its own APIs and uses different programming languages. Therefore, we need to consider that our code base may run on any device. To make sure about this, we can use the JavaScript engine as it runs on any platform. You can use **Cordova** (`http://cordova.apache.org/`) to understand how to build apps using JavaScript. Cordova is a JavaScript framework based on every device's APIs. You can use **PhoneGap** (`http://phonegap.com/`) or **Meteor** (`https://www.meteor.com/`) to build smartphone apps with JavaScript.

Running web servers

You probably have heard of web servers. The server is used to broadcast websites. You can rule your server using JavaScript. JavaScript can handle all the operations and confirms the security of your domains. You can use **Node.js** (`https://nodejs.org/`) to run the simplest web server. To know more about the JavaScript web servers, you can take a look at `https://www.firebase.com/`. You may have basic knowledge of JavaScript, which is needed to perform the tasks in a web server. Building a web server with other framework may have a high cost; however, with JavaScript, you can do it for free, You don't even need to buy any software for this.

Running Ruby and Python

JavaScript also can be used to run **Python** or **Ruby** on your browsers with few lines of external code. You may include the running environment of these programming languages on your browsers by adding libraries. To learn more about library including and running the codes of Ruby and Python on your browser, you may take a look at `https://www.firebase.com`.

Writing OS-independent desktop applications

Since JavaScript is platform-independent, you can build web applications with the help of JavaScript and run them on any platform. Users on any platform can run the JavaScript-based apps on their browsers. You can even make desktop applications using JavaScript. Take a look at `http://appjs.com/` and `http://electron.atom.io/` to make your first desktop application based on JavaScript.

Web scraping and screenshotting

The technique of extracting information from a website is called web scraping. To learn more about web scraping you can head to `http://www.webscraper.io/`. JavaScript can help you with web scraping. You can take a look at `http://nrabinowitz.github.io/pjscrape/` to learn more about web scraping with JavaScript.

You can take a look at `https://html2canvas.hertzen.com/` to learn more about screenshotting of your website. Screenshotting can be done using JavaScript.

Web analytics

Sometimes, you may need to know who is visiting your website, from which IP address is your website regularly being visited, which country does the visitor belong to, and a lot more information about tracking the visitors. All of this information can be obtained using JavaScript.

Responsive and interactive contents

With JavaScript, you can make responsive and interactive contents on your website and web application. You can take a look at `http://beta.rallyinteractive.com/`, `http://www.unfold.no/`, `http://www.2advanced.com/`, and `http://www.newquest.fr/` to see how they made their website responsive and interactive using JavaScript.

Animation

The awesome thing about JavaScript is that you can do animation with it. There are a lot of cool JavaScript animation libraries. Take a look at `http://greensock.com/gsap` to learn more about **GreenSock**, a famous JavaScript animation library. There is another famous library for JavaScript animation named **Velocity.js** (`http://julian.com/research/velocity/`).

Creating cookies

You may have heard about web cookies. Consider that you input your username and password on a website, there popped up an alert stating that you can save the username and information. You hit **Remember Password** and the information is then stored in your computer as cookie. Your web cookies are created with JavaScript. The web cookies are important for a website to load faster. You can learn more about web cookies from `http://www.allaboutcookies.org/cookies/`.

Awesome JavaScript examples

There are few websites to visualize the latest JavaScript works by users. One of them is `http://creativejs.com/`. You will also find some tutorials there. `CreativeJS.com` is the go-to place to find exciting JavaScript demos, projects, games, and anything else that they consider to be awesome. They've got a whole team there to bring you the best of what's out there. The following screenshot is the homepage of `CreativeJS.com`:

Here are a few examples of JavaScript projects with their links:

- **Awesome calculator**: The following calculator was built with JavaScript, HTML, and CSS. The animation of the glowing button is done by JavaScript:

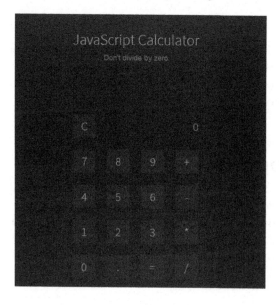

This calculator can be found at `http://codepen.io/giana/pen/GJMBEv`.

- **Drag and drop**: You can drag one block and drop it on another block with your mouse. The dragging is done using JavaScript. The following is a screenshot of this project:

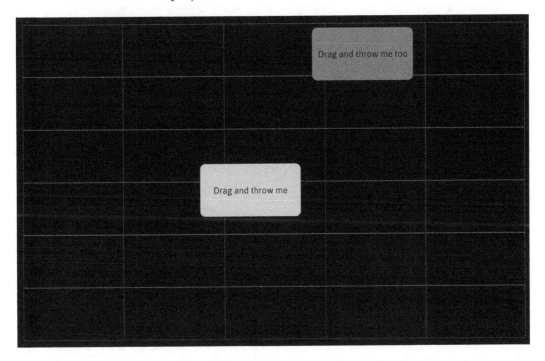

This project can be found at `http://greensock.com/draggable`.

- **Random maze generator**: You built a game called Rat-man, where you needed to draw a map for the cats and the rat to move. The path was like a maze. The following link will generate a random maze for you. I hope you pay attention to the JavaScript that they used there:

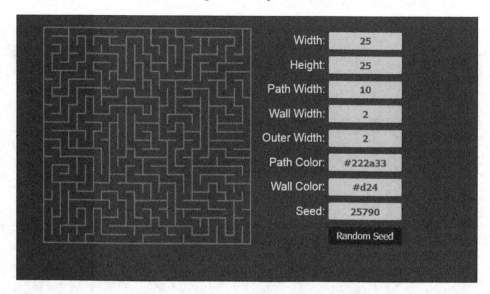

This game can be found at `http://codepen.io/GabbeV/pen/viAec`.

- **Particle joining**: You can play with joining particles at `http://codepen.io/garyconstable/pen/fEoLz`. This particles' movements are controlled by JavaScript. The following is a screenshot of this project:

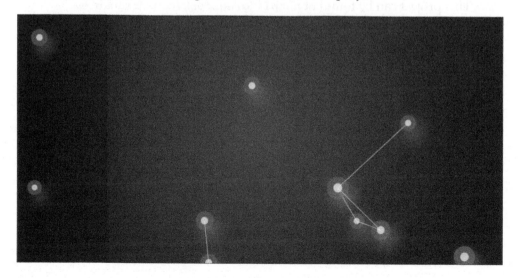

- **Tearable cloth**: If you want to make a simulation of a cloth, you can go to the link `http://codepen.io/dissimulate/pen/KrAwx` and play with the piece of cloth here. The motion of the cloth is controlled by JavaScript. The following is the screenshot of this project:

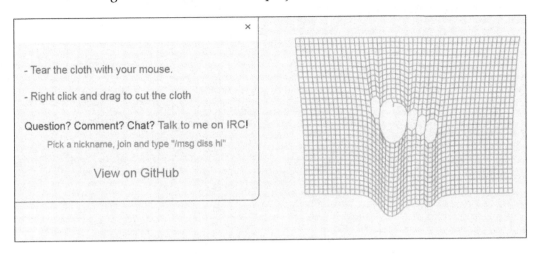

- **Neon thing**: You can use the following thing on your website as button. I hope you learn how its code works. The following is a screenshot of this project:

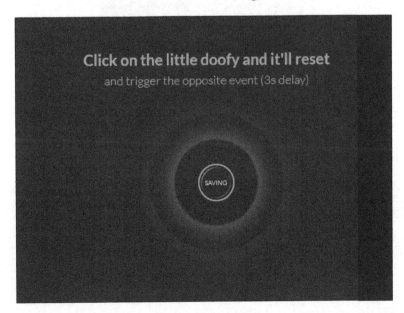

This project can be found at `http://codepen.io/simeydotme/details/Gzfuh`.

- **Smartphone submenu**: If you are thinking about making a smartphone application with JavaScript, you will definitely need a submenu for the app. You can go to `http://codepen.io/berdejitendra/pen/AgEzJ` and learn how to make a cool submenu for your mobile application. The following is a screenshot of this project:

- **3D Solar System**: If you love astronomy and the motion of planets, the link `http://codepen.io/juliangarnier/pen/idhuG` will bring you an awesome visualization of the neighboring planets and their information. All the dynamic elements were created using JavaScript. The following is a screenshot of this project:

Summary

We are at the end of the book. This book is not everything on JavaScript. It is the starting of JavaScript. I hope you enjoyed the book and practiced all the exercises and projects that were discussed in the book. I hope that you will visit the websites in this chapter and observe the codes of each project in order to learn more about JavaScript. I hope that someday you will create your own dynamic website with the help of JavaScript, build a smartphone app with JavaScript, and you may also be able to build a robot using JavaScript. You never know!

I hope that you have learned a lot of awesome things to explore with JavaScript; now it's your time to experiment with code and play with JavaScript. Don't worry if anything goes wrong. Keep in mind:

> *"It's not at all important to get it right the first time. It's vitally important to get it right the last time."*

> *– Andrew Hunt and David Thomas*

Index

Symbol

3D games
creating, with JavaScript 157
reference link 157

A

abstraction 148
AngularJS
URL 151
animation
creating, with JavaScript 159
Arduino 157
arithmetic operators
about 19
addition 19
division 21
modulus 22-24
multiplication 21
subtraction 20
assignment operators 27, 28
Atom
about 2
advantages 9
installing 3, 4
keyboard shortcuts 8
URL 3

B

Battleship game
code, executing 73-82
creating 65
CSS code, writing 69

game rules 66, 67
HTML code, writing 68
JavaScript code, writing 69-72
bitwise operators 30
blur() method 92, 93
build-in objects 12
Business Narrative Markup Language (BNML) 33
buttons
adding, to HTML web page 55

C

canvas
circle, drawing 100, 101
implementing 97
JavaScript, adding 98
line, drawing 99
liner gradient, drawing 101, 102
rectangle, drawing 98, 99
canvas, Rat-man
app.constants.js file 135
app.key_handler.js file 129
app.movement_functions.js file 130-133
drawing 129
Cascading Style Sheets (CSS)
about 33, 46
applying 46, 47
change() method 91
Chrome Developer Tools
advantages 9
using 4
clock
creating 102-111

J

JavaScript
  adding, for canvas 98
  as programming language 155
  browser support 155
  examples 160
  methods, using 52-54
  online references 155
  use cases 156
  using, on HTML page 48, 49
JavaScript developer 156
Joint Photographic Experts Group
        (JPG/JPEG) 43
jQuery
  about 83
  code, explaining 88
  installing 84-87
  methods 89
  URL 84
jSelect 83

K

keydown() method 90
keyup() method 90
keywords 12

L

line
  drawing, in canvas 99
liner gradient
  drawing, in canvas 101, 102
load() method 89
logical operators 29, 30
loops
  about 61
  for loop 61, 62
  while loop 61-63

M

Meteor
  URL 158
methods
  using 52-54

methods, jQuery
  about 89
  blur() method 92, 93
  change() method 91
  focus() method 92, 93
  keydown() method 90
  keyup() method 90
  load() method 89
  resize() method 93
  scroll() method 93, 94
modulus (%) operator 23

N

NodeBots
  URL 157
Node.js
  URL 158

O

object-oriented programming (OOP)
  about 141
  reference link 148
objects 141
Opera Binary Markup
        Language (OBML) 33
operators
  about 25
  assignment operators 27, 28
  comparison operators 29, 30
  decrement operators 25-27
  increment operators 25-27
  logical operators 29, 30
OS-independent desktop applications
  reference links 158
  writing, JavaScript used 158

P

Pac-Man 113
PhoneGap
  URL 158
polymorphism 148
Portable Network Graphics (PNG) 43
Python
  running, JavaScript used 158

R

Rat-man
about 113
canvas, drawing 129
functionalities, adding 117
images, adding 125
playing 136-139
user interface, creating 114-116
rectangle
drawing, in canvas 98, 99
resize() method 93
responsive and interactive contents
creating 159
references 159
robotics
with JavaScript 157
Ruby
running, JavaScript used 158

S

screenshotting 159
scroll() method 93, 94
smartphone apps
creating, with JavaScript 158
software development kit (SDK) 1
Standard Generalized Markup Language (SGML) 33
Static website 1
switch-case statement 59, 60
SyntaxError 17
Systems Biology Markup Language (SBML) 33

U

Uncaught SyntaxError 11

use cases, JavaScript

3D games 157
about 156
animation 159
cookies, creating 159
OS-independent desktop applications, writing 158
Python, running 158
responsive and interactive contents 159
robotics 157
Ruby, running 158
screenshotting 159
smartphone apps, creating 158
web analytics 159
web scraping 159
web servers, running 158

V

variables
about 12
example 13-17
Velocity.js
URL 159
Virtual Human Markup Language (VHML) 33

W

web analytics
with JavaScript 159
web cookies
reference link 159
web scraping
about 159
URL 159
web servers
running, JavaScript used 158
while loop 61-63

Thank you for buying
JavaScript Projects for Kids

About Packt Publishing

Packt, pronounced 'packed', published its first book, *Mastering phpMyAdmin for Effective MySQL Management*, in April 2004, and subsequently continued to specialize in publishing highly focused books on specific technologies and solutions.

Our books and publications share the experiences of your fellow IT professionals in adapting and customizing today's systems, applications, and frameworks. Our solution-based books give you the knowledge and power to customize the software and technologies you're using to get the job done. Packt books are more specific and less general than the IT books you have seen in the past. Our unique business model allows us to bring you more focused information, giving you more of what you need to know, and less of what you don't.

Packt is a modern yet unique publishing company that focuses on producing quality, cutting-edge books for communities of developers, administrators, and newbies alike. For more information, please visit our website at www.packtpub.com.

About Packt Open Source

In 2010, Packt launched two new brands, Packt Open Source and Packt Enterprise, in order to continue its focus on specialization. This book is part of the Packt Open Source brand, home to books published on software built around open source licenses, and offering information to anybody from advanced developers to budding web designers. The Open Source brand also runs Packt's Open Source Royalty Scheme, by which Packt gives a royalty to each open source project about whose software a book is sold.

Writing for Packt

We welcome all inquiries from people who are interested in authoring. Book proposals should be sent to author@packtpub.com. If your book idea is still at an early stage and you would like to discuss it first before writing a formal book proposal, then please contact us; one of our commissioning editors will get in touch with you.

We're not just looking for published authors; if you have strong technical skills but no writing experience, our experienced editors can help you develop a writing career, or simply get some additional reward for your expertise.

Object-Oriented JavaScript
Second Edition
ISBN: 978-1-84969-312-7   Paperback: 382 pages

Learn everything you need to know about OOJS in this comprehensive guide

1. Think in JavaScript.

2. Make object-oriented programming accessible and understandable to web developers.

3. Apply design patterns to solve JavaScript coding problems.

4. Learn coding patterns that unleash the unique power of the language.

JavaScript at Scale
ISBN: 978-1-78528-215-7   Paperback: 266 pages

Build enduring JavaScript applications with scaling insights from the front-line of JavaScript development

1. Design and implement JavaScript application architectures that scale from a number of perspectives, such as addressability, configurability, and performance.

2. Understand common JavaScript scaling pitfalls and how to tackle them through practical, real-world, solutions and strategies.

3. Learn techniques to deliver reusable architectures that stand the test of time.

Please check **www.PacktPub.com** for information on our titles

Made in the USA
Columbia, SC
24 November 2018